Why & How We, the People, Must Remove Trump

R.G.Coleman, Ph.D.

Books by R.G. Coleman, Ph.D.

Is Your Prescription Killing You?
The People v George "Dubya" Bush
The Governor's Fingerprints
A Mom's Perfect Murder?
Alice's Wonderland
*God: The Torah & Bible for Smart and Funny People
        Only*
*Trump's Troops Revolt Against Republican Party's
        Betrayal*
.Justice for Baby Josh
*Good Dad – Bad Mom – The Criminalization of a
        Father's Paternal Instincts – Part One*
*Good Dad – Bad Mom – The Criminalization of a
        Father's Paternal Instincts – Part Two*
Johnny Carson, Ted Williams, and Me
Dirty Judges – America's Broken Judicial System

By RG as Jocelyn Otis Coleman

My One-Night Stand With God's Assassin
My Daughter's Keeper

Dedicated To

*Barack Obama, who suffered Trump's
mutinous slander and libel with dignity
and class,*

*Hillary Clinton, who but for Trump's
slander and libel would be the first
woman president of the United States*

*John Dean, for his role as America's
current Tom Paine.*

....without their knowledge or consent

"These are the times that try men's (and women's) soul. The summer soldier and sunshine patriot will, in this crisis, shrink from the service of their country; but he (and she) that stands it now, deserves the love and thanks of every man and woman.

(Trump's) Tyranny, like hell, is not easily conquered; yet we have this consolation with us, that the harder the conflict, the more glorious the triumph. What we obtain too cheap, we esteem too lightly: it is dearness only that gives everything its value." -- *Thomas Paine*

By What Authority, or Who the Hell is This R.G. Coleman, Ph.D. Writing Why and How to Remove Trump?\

Fair enough. Let us count the ways. (1) I have a Ph.D. in psychology, trained and qualified to diagnose mental disorders. (2) I have made mental health diagnoses as part of some 3,500-4,000 evaluations among patients/clients in hospitals, prisons, schools, institutions, and mental health centers, for state agencies, private companies, and individuals. (3) It has been obvious to me, after hours of observing Donald J. Trump in a variety of "natural settings," versus contrived office settings, listening to hours of his speeches, and reading hundreds of his tweets that Donald Trump meets, or exceeds the criteria for Narcissistic Personality Disorder, as described in The *Diagnostic and Statistical Manual of Mental Disorders* (DSM – IV and V) and as such, represents a clear and present danger to the internal and external security of the United States.

In 1964, *Fact Magazine* published a survey of psychiatrists as to the mental health of Barry Goldwater, Republican presidential candidate. Goldwater lost the election, but won a 1$75,000 libel law suit against *Fact Magazine.*

Based on that law suit, in 1973, the American Psychiatric Association and the

American Psychological Association enacted the so called "Goldwater Rule," a ruse to regain control of its straying members by decreeing, "that it is unethical for a psychiatrist to offer a professional opinion unless he, or she, has conducted an examination and has been granted proper authorization for such statements."

Not only was the Goldwater Rule self-serving then, it is irrelevant now, to wit, since Trump's campaign began on June 16, 2015, Trump has so dominated the media that his public behavior, speeches, and tweets have been so prolific that a one-two hour psychiatric or psychological examination of Trump would be as necessary as a third wing on a bird.

When the choice is between exercising dutiful professional responsibility to preserve, protect and defend America, versus an allegiance to the American Psychiatric and Psychological Association's concerned with exercising their arbitrary authority and control over its members, the inexorable choice must be the United States of America.

So, I waited for a psychiatrist or psychologist to promulgate the relationship between Trump's Narcissistic Personality and his, (a) Promotion of a treacherous, fraudulent, and treasonous "Populism", (b) Neo-Nazism, (c) (c) Racism, (d) Persecution of Muslims and their religion, (e) Persecution of immigrants, (f) Promotion of insurrection, hate, divisiveness -- of an internecine war between his 33% and the 66%, (g) Treasonous, mutinous, arbitrary, and personal trashing of all things Obama, regardless of its value to Americans, (h) Contemptuous ignorance of, and disrespect for, the Constitution of the United Sates, as campaigner Trump,' (i) Slanderous and libelous, statements and tweets, for example, :"Killer' Hillary" "Convict Hillary," and similar personal attacks on those who opposed him, for which he should have been sued, (j) Fraudulent campaign promises he knew, or should have known, he could not keep, to wit, "Repeal and Replace Obamacare," – "I will build a wall and make Mexico pay for it," -- tasks assigned to Congress by the Constitution, NOT the President, (k) Violation of the letter and intent of the Constitutional promise of a "fair and impartial federal judiciary," by nominating and supporting a known ultra-Conservative, Scalia-zealots as U S Supreme Court judge, thereby affixing the Pro-Conservative stamp of approval on **all** future Federal Court rulings, (l) De facto *coup d'état,* replacing the Republic with a Neo-Nazi/Neo-Nationalist Die Fuhrer named Donald J. Trump, (m) Vitiating the Federal Government by reigning as Die Fuhrer via "Executive Orders" and propaganda, (n) Die Fuhrer administrating foreign policy according to his personal likes or dislikes of the foreign leader, (o) Bullying tactics with foreign leaders and his refusal to honor past treaties, both based on his personal whims and prejudices, which threatens the world's stability, and the security of Americans, (p) Alienation of other countries – Trump's international pomposity incurring the displeasure of friend and foe, (q) Mussolini-like braggadocio, and provocative personal attacks on the leader of North Korea causing world-wide fear of a nuclear war, (r) Trickle-down economics the same as lead to Reagan's Not-So-Great-Depression – unemployment 10.8 % and most bank failings since 1929, (s) Policy of deregulation the same as Bush II's which caused the meltdown of 2007, (t) Betrayal of his "base' by giving the biggest tax break to corporations, less than tax rate for individuals thereby widening the gap between the 10% and the 90%, (u) Pardoning of convicted Gestapo Sheriff "Joe" Arpaio and his support for another Neo-Nazi, Alabama's Roy Moore, reveals his true allegiance to Neo-Nazi/Neo-Nationalist governance, and (v) Arrogant presumption the Government of the United States is a company Trump owns, its workers, his employees, sworn to indulge Donald in his every instance of self-love and grandiosity.

Therefore, absent known public psychiatric or psychological analysis as to the deleterious effect of Trump's Narcissistic Personality Disorder on the Republic, consumed by fear that, Trump's presidency has 1930's Nazi Germany as its mentor, confronted with the reality, that the so-called *New York Times*, *Washington Post* , NPR, *et al*, experts and pundits, failed to predict Trump's election, and who, still remain ignorant of Trump's mental condition, and its ruinous effect   on American domestic and foreign policy, "nobody knows my name" R,G. Coleman, Ph.D., reluctantly wrote, *Why and How We, the People, Must Remove Trump.*

How Trump Happened

In 2000, a corrupt Conservative Republican United States Supreme Court, boasting of its "States Rights" bias, violated the State of Florida's election laws for the sole purpose of installing one of their own -- Conservative Republican George "Dubya". Bush, as President of the United States. (Supreme Court Judge Clarence Thomas, appointed by Bush's father, should have recused himself, but didn't)

Instead of taking to the streets to demand the Conservative Republican judges be impeached, that the Court's illegal and unconstitutional decision to anoint "Dubya" President be declared null and void, and the *de facto* winner of the popular vote, Democrat Al Gore, be awarded the presidency, we, the people waxed. wimps.

Furthermore, **Florida's corrupt, crooked, Supervisor of Elections, Kathryn Harris, <u>who was also Dubya's Florida Republican Campaign Chairperson,</u> conspired with "Dubya's" brother Jeb Bush, Governor of Florida, to purge the names of thousands of male African-American voters, and Dubya's Texas offered Florida the names of 5,000 African-American males with criminal records, to be illegally purged from the eligible voter rolls,** (*The Best Democracy Money Can Buy,-* Greg Palast), we the people emitted not so much as a whimper of protest.

The price of our failure to take up arms against this sea of corrupt Supreme Court Conservative Republican judges, a corrupt Florida Supervisor of Elections and a crooked Florida Governor, would be eight years of a corrupt, incompetent, Conservative, Republican President – Narcissistic Personality Disorder George "Dubya" Bush, who would lie – give perjured testimony to the Congress of the United States – an impeachable offense -- and the United Nations – an impeachable offense, for the sole fraudulent purpose to "take out" Saddam Hussein – an impeachable offense – when "Dubya" had already invaded Afghanistan under fraudulent pretence – an impeachable offense.

7,000 of us have been killed fighting "Dubya's" two fraudulent wars, thousands more of us lost arms, legs, and our sanity.

The number of Iraqi and Afghanistan women and children killed ranges from 300,000 to 600,000, and counting.

At home, as a direct result of Conservative Republican President "Dubya's: UNREGULATED banks and mortgage companies, we suffered the third of three depressions during the presidencies of three Conservative Republicans – Hoover, Reagan, and "Dubya.", Millions of us lost our jobs and had our homes foreclosed.

And how did Dubya help us? **During the first WEEKEND of Dubya's Depression, he and his Secretary of the Treasury, Henry Paulson – former Chief Executive Officer of Goldman Sachs – one of the Investment banks he and**

Dubya rescued, rushed through a $700 BILLION BAILOUT!

And for the rest of us, millions now unemployed and our homes foreclosed, Conservative Republican President Bush II dismisses our plight by offering the same insouciant solution Marie Antoinette offered the French peasants – "Let them eat cake!"

From the millions of us victimized by "Dubya's" two illegal wars and his Not So Great Depression, would be those exploited by Conservative Republican Donald J. Trump's Hiterleresque propaganda that the years of their discontent were not caused by Conservative Republican George "Dubya" Bush, 2000-2008, but by the current Democratic and first-ever African American President, Barack Obama. (*Trump's Troops Revolt Against Republican Party's Betrayal*, R.G. Coleman – Amazon)

Wearing the hat of "Populist" over the hood of a closet KKK'er, Trump conned the unemployed that: (1) He would "create 10 million jobs over 10 yearsl" Presidents can't and don't create jobs, they enforce labor and worker protection laws , and that (2) He "would be the best jobs President God ever created!"

First, with each war to decide which God is the true God, the emerging answer being "No God," Trump's claim that he will be the "greatest jobs President God ever created," is based on Trump's delusions of grandeur, not God's existence. Second, if there were a "job's God," FDR, NOT Donald J. Trump, would be "best."

Then too, Trump would be the gratuitous benefactor of eight years of the Conservative

Republican Congress's sabotage of every nomination, every proposal, bill, law, and program offered by President Obama, regardless of its merits or benefit to us, the people.

Exploitive, unprincipled, ruthless, candidate Trump, not only climbs aboard Congress's "Bury Obama" bandwagon, but seizes the reigns,

Fast forward ten short years. While still trying to recover from one Conservative Republican's debauched narcissistic presidency, we find ourselves -- déjà vu – governed by another Narcissistic Conservative Republican President, whose Hitleresque Big Lies, propaganda, criminal slander and libel of his opponents, treacherous control of the media by promulgating fraudulent, outrageous, shameless statements and tweets, ("Fake News"), making fraudulent campaign promises, exploiting the anger and fear caused by Dubya's Depression, and aided and abetted by the criminal intervention of Russian President Putin, all while another Democratic presidential candidate and winner of the popular vote is denied the Office of President of the United States

As happened in January 2001, on January 20, 2017, we the people of the United States were once again victims of another Conservative Republican, debauched, narcissistic, President, different from Dubya only in being more narcissistic, more treacherous, and more dangerous – Dubya on steroids.

Trump's medieval menacing candidacy also had time on its side. In those 10 years, America had further regressed into its dark age of post- World War II extreme neo-Conservatism, begun somewhat innocently by Republican Eisenhower's 1954 Executive Order interjecting the words, "under God" into the previously secular Pledge of Allegiance, and his "domino theory" of war, leading to lost wars in Korea, and Vietnam.

Next, Eisenhower's vice president, now President Nixon's treacherous "law and order' *modus operandi* divided Americans into "bad-guys" -- civil rights activists and Vietnam protesters versus "good guys" – neo-Conservative "lock-em up and throw away the key," "three strikes you're out," maximum sentences, the NRA as a government agency, and abortion of a pre-human fetus is murder but the death of a fully human inmate isn't.

Nixon's even more treacherous "Southern Strategy" violated the fundamental principle of "separation of church and state," and further divided America by converting the "religious (wrong) rights" into politicians, (Falwell's Moral Majority in 1979 – neither moral nor the majority) and politicians into the religious evangelical Right – an early Jimmy Carter, Orrin Hatch, Jesse Helms, Ronald Reagan, George Dubya Bush and, most recently Protestant Pope Pence.

Former class "B" Hollywood actor, Screen Actors Guild's leftist president, Conservative extremist hand-picked by Orange County, California John Birchers, ex-Governor of California, neo-Conservative poster boy, then President of the United States Ronald Reagan, charmed – conned America's media into pandering to, rather than panning, Reagan's "Reign of Errors" -- eight years of "rickle-down economics" – lower taxes for the rich and de-regulation of business, leading to the worst Depression since the crash of "29" – unemployment 10.8%. the most bank failings since '29" lowest production rate since 1934, and America became debtor nation for first time since World War I. (Reagan invades super-power Granada for a weekend Super Bowl War, to deflect attention from his botched "trickle-down" economics policies.)

Reagan sends Marines into Beirut Lebanon, promising they would be home in 30 days. A year later, October, 1983, 240 of those Marines and support troops are killed by a truck bomber as they slept in their barracks.

No shouts of "Beirut," in 1990, 1994, 2000, 2004, 2008, 2012, but Trump shouts "Benghazi" in 2016.

Reagan violates domestic and International law by selling arms to Iran, (also an impeachable offence), in exchange for which Iran would pay ransom (an impeachable offense) for the release of American hostages in Lebanon. The price of the arms is grossly inflated so that the excess profits can be diverted to the Contras (an impeachable offense) in their fight against the communist Sandinistas in Nicaragua.

The Iran-Contra scandal, for which Reagan is ultimately culpable, results in Reagan's fall from grace, his impeachment, and exclusion from retirement checks. Right?

Not exactly. Already disgraced by Nixon, Conservative Republicans circled the wagons, conspired with the Republican Senator John Tower, head of the presidentially appointed commission, and the Conservative media to let avuncular Ronnie ride off into the sunset, his retirement check in hand, and not so much as a scratch on Reagan's exalted status as Conservative's poster boy,

On the other hand, these same neo-Conservative missionaries -- corrupt zealots everyone -- rush to impeach President Bill Clinton for making the rookie mistake of not citing his Fifth Amendment right to refuse to testify against himself, to the present, where Trump, no student of history and without a conscience, slanders Hillary Clinton as "Killer Hillary. and "Convict Hillary,"'' with no arrest or conviction of either.

As can be plainly gleaned, neo-Conservatives, as Hillary noted 20 years ago, "They (Neo -Conservatives) go for the jugular," being guided by three codes of conduct: (1) "The best lie wins – the bigger the lie the better, (see Hitler's *Mein Kamph*). (2) The ends justifies the means, and (3) Conservative causes come before Party, before Country and before God.

To that list Trump adds and practices, "Say and do that whatever captures the most media attention, no matter how outrageous, how false, how slanderous, or how injurious to the person being attacked.

So it was that Trump happened upon eight years of Conservative, Republican, racist, hate-mongering, personal attacks on America's first African-American President, his Affordable

Healthcare Act, his environmental/clean energy and global-warming initiatives, his war ending, and economic recovery successes, so that by the time Mitch McConnell, House leaders Boehner and Ryan had worked to defeat all things Obama, it was too easy for a "Take no prisoners" mentally disordered, and man without a conscience – Donald J. Trump to evict the Obama's from the White House..

To quote Reagan, but in a far different context, "Government is not the solution; government is the problem," -- the problem being the Congressional Republican-controlled government, (excepting Senate warriors McCain, Collins, Murkowski), which has repeatedly sacrificed the good of the American people for the "bad" of obstructing Obama and the Democrats. These Neo-Conservatives are, as John Dean so aptly described them "Conservatives without consciences," – not only useless, but obstructive in our efforts to save the Republic from itself by removing Trump as President

Democrats, having been "processed out" of the process – their wings clipped by Mitch McConnell's change in the rules of engagement – 51%, not 60% to pass laws and bills, bequeath to us, the people, the task of righting this wrong of Trump being President or, once again, being the government's victims;

If, as Lincoln promised, the government of the United States is the government of the people, by the people and for the people, our cause, being just, honorable and patriotic, must prevail. If not that type of government, we have another cause, more patriotic and more desperate than this one, to engage.

 # **<u>Count One</u>**
<u>Trump Committed Multiple Acts of Fraud and Fraud in the Inducement to Get Voters to Vote for Him.</u>

We will show that Donald J. Trump obtained the presidency of the United States by fraudulent means -- the actionable offenses of fraud in the inducement, and fraud.

For example, Trump fraudulently induced some of us to vote for him by: (1)Making promises he knew, or should have known, were the province of Congress, not the President, and therefore promises he should not have made and could not keep, to wit, "I will Repeal and Replace Obamacare," "I will build a wall across the Mexican border and make Mexico pay for it," and, I will " bring manufacturing jobs back to the US -- I'm going to be the greatest jobs president God ever made."

Specific evidence of Trump's fraudulent inducements to vote for him include, but are not limited to, those campaign promises made on October 22, 2016, as his "Contract with the American voter," which won him just under three million votes less than Hillary Clinton. For example;

Trump: <u>"I will make America great again,"</u>

Trump implies that Democrats Obama and Clinton, but not the real culprit – fellow

Conservative Republican George Dubya Bush -- caused the United States to spiral downward, and that he alone, *uber alles*, Donald J. Trump, untrained, unqualified, inexperienced, ill-tempered, and with a debilitating mental disorder, will "make American great again.".

This is a classic example of Trump's deluded grandiosity, omnipotence, and false sense of self-importance. --"I alone above all others – not Rubio, not Cruz, not Kasich, *et al*, and certainly not "Convict Hillary" who's going to jail, or "Bernie, who couldn't even beat "Killer" Hillary," will save America from itself, begging the question, who, will save us from deluded Donald?

But, Trump's fraudulent promises aside, we must be alarmed that Trump's promises are driven by his perverse narcissism – his compulsion to create a crowd of admirers who will admire him as he admires himself – the presidency of the United States merely the setting for Trump's treacherous charade.

Trump's promise to "make America great again," while deliberately vague and unverifiable, nevertheless fraudulently induced voters to believe Trump had the power and authority he knew, or should have known he didn't have

Trump: "<u>I will build a wall across the Mexican border and make Mexico pay for it,</u>"

Trump knew, or should have known the President does not, and cannot, appropriate the funds to build the wall. As any 6th grader learns, funding is the function of the Legislative Branch of government, not the Executive Branch. No congressional approval, no wall.

Furthermore, Trump has no authority to force Mexico to do anything, including picking up the tab for the wall,

More grandiose polices and promises hatched in the brain stem of deluded Donald to satiate his narcissism – as if the relationship between Mexico and the United States is irrelevant!

More unreasonable expectations –based on Trump's grandiose presumption that the President of Mexico is inferior to Trump, and will therefore automatically comply with Trump's demand that he pay for the wall. By promising to build a wall, not his to build, Trump fraudulently induced voters to vote for him.

Trump: "By bringing manufacturing jobs back to the US, I'm going to be the greatest jobs president God ever made."

Oh? There are many who deify Trump simply because they believe Trump's promise of bringing manufacturing jobs back to the US is to help workers who lost their factory jobs due to Dubya's "Not-So- Great Depression," and not because for years, US companies have been plundering Mexico, China, India, and Bangladesh for cheap labor

Now, it seems Trump has again duped voters. Not jobs for unemployed factory workers but instead, Donald is just looking for another way to prop up his delusion that he's the "greatest" – this time the "greatest jobs president God ever made," which begs the questions, who did Trump replace? FDR?

Reality check: (a) Manufacturing jobs have been declining since the end of World War II – nothing like a good old ground war to get full employment and keep the grave-digger's union members happy. (b) Trump's capitalist cousins in manufacturing chase cheap labor like sailors in port chase hookers.   (3) No company ever "created" jobs. Other than FDR, no President did either. Companies hire workers only to profit from their labor – make the company more money than the company would make without the worker. Case in point: Textile mills abandoned New England for cheap non-union labor in the South, in turn, abandoning the south for cheaper labor in Bangladesh.

So it would follow. as night follows day that deluded Donald can self-anoint himself "the greatest jobs president God ever made," by getting American workers to work for a lower wages than workers in Bangladesh, China, India, or Mexico. (I want to attend the rally where Trump tells his unemployed base that their factory wages are going from $12-$20 dollars an hour to $1.00 -2.00 a day..

By making the promise to bring back manufacturing jobs in such numbers as to be declared "the greatest jobs President God ever made," Trump fraudulently induced voters to vote for him.

Trump: <u>"I will appoint a special prosecutor to investigate Hillary Clinton, and to investigate the investigation"</u>

More narcissistic fanaticizing! If Trump had done his homework, he wouldn't embarrass himself AND the Presidency by abusing the Office of President of the United States to pursue his paranoid, personal, and private peeves.

More importantly, the slanderous, nasty, fraudulent slurs Trump makes about Hillary Clinton exposes more about Trump than about Hillary – that Trump is a self-absorbed, mean-spirited, vindictive, arrogant, bully, without a conscience, who will shamelessly slander anyone to get elected.

Furthermore, if Trump must make it appear as though Secretary of State Hillary Clinton was responsible for the two terrorist attacks on American facilities in Libya in 2012, which left an Ambassador and two American CIA contractors dead, then Trump must condemn Republican President Reagan, posthumously for the death of 240 marines killed in Lebanon a year after Reagan promised their families they would be home in 30 days.

Following the same line of reasoning, the Conservative Republican Congress must charge and convict Bush II for the deaths of 7.000 American soldiers killed, and thousands more left armless and legless -- "wounded warriors" fighting "Dubya's" two dirty" and criminally fraudulent wars in Afghanistan and Iraq based on Dubya's and Cheney's perjured testimony made to the American mothers, and fathers, of those killed.

Oh, it's Hillary's e-mails for which Trump demands an investigation?

Not that Trump would listen, but someone needs his ear -- his lying, slanderous tweets, and alleged shady communication with Putin which may well make Hillary's e-mails read like her love letters to Bill.

By promising to appoint a special prosecutor to investigate Hillary Clinton Trump deceived voters that his slanderous claims of "Killer Hillary," and "Convict Hillary" had a basis in fact, which he knew, or should have known, to be false, thereby fraudulently inducing voters to vote for him

Trump: "I'm going to cancel every needless job-killing regulation and put a moratorium on new regulations until our economy gets back on its feet."

Narcissistic sound and fury signifying nothing, other than Trump's delusions of grandiosity -- his illusion of omnipotence, unsupported by reality.

The job of deciding which regulations are "needless job killing regulations" falls under Secretary of Labor's job description. NOT Donald's

Historically, American companies have always decried any and all labor regulations as "needless job-killing regulations,' from the child-labor laws of the 1830's, to equal pay for women, to minimum wage regulations in 2017.

Every new regulation is always countered by businesses threatening lay-offs or closing down and moving to Mexico and beyond -- loyalty to America and concern for the American worker, be damned!

Only 71, and already Trump suffers from memory loss. Incipient Alzheimer's?

By the way, "getting the "economy back on its feet," – recover from Republican President Dubya's UNREGULATED mortgage banking companies – Dubya's "Not-So-Great-Depression, -- fell on the shoulders of Democrat President Obama, just as Hoover's Great Depression fell on FDR's shoulders and Regan's secreted depression fell on Bill Clinton's.

A non-narcissistic Trump, would have thanked Obama and sought his advice and counsel.

Deregulated companies and the Republican politicians who represent them, would have 10 year-olds working 10 hours a day in factories, women making 50% of what men make doing the same job, unions would be outlawed, employers could hire, or refuse to hire, and fire workers at will, there would be no OSHA, no EPA, and no Workmen's Compensation. The worker who is disabled or killed by brown lung or asbestos, or otherwise injured or killed on the job, should have been more careful.

In any event, as an employer, thereby having a conflict of interest in dealing with labor matters, and despite his narcissistic claim that he is entitled to automatic compliance with his fantasies of power and control, Donald still doesn't get to usurp the title and functions of the Secretary of Labor.

By promising to eliminate all "job-killing regulations," which Trump knew, or should have known, was outside Trump's job description, Trump fraudulently induced voters to vote for him

Trump: <u>"I'm not going to cut Social Security like every other Republican and I'm not going to cut Medicare or Medicaid. "</u>

Donald's narcissistic gratuitous concessions lose their luster in the reality that Trump doesn't cut Social Security Medicare, or Medicaid – Congress -- the Republicans he just derided, and the Democrats he incessantly insults, determine the fate of all three.

By promising not to cut Social Security, Trump deceived voters that he had authority over Social Security, he knew, or should have known, his didn't have, thereby fraudulently inducing voters to vote for him

Trump: <u>"I'm expanding vocational and technical education."</u>

First, Trump takes over the State Department in dealing with Mexico, takes over Homeland Security by mandating a wall, takes over Congress by amending the Constitution, the Labor Department by deregulating labor laws, the job of the Attorney General by appointing a Special Prosecutor, the Republican House of Representatives by not cutting Social Security,

Medicare and Medicaid, and now the Department of Education by trashing Common Core and expanding vocational and technical education. (Federal or State?).

Oh, Donald is just keeping his campaign promise of reducing the size of the Federal Government, rendering it to a staff of ONE -- Donald Trump?!

A king without courtesans – military dictator without soldiers, demagogue without his subjects, Company owner without employees?

By promising to expand vocational and technical education, Trump deceived voters that he had the authority to do so, when Trump knew, or should have known, he had no such authority, thereby fraudulently inducing voters to vote for him

Trump: <u>"I'm expanding two -four-year vocational technical education,"</u>

His intrusion into education is no more profane than his choice for Education Secretary DeVos, who like Trump, is arrogant, rich, with a business-background, a Republican, with no more experience, training, and knowledge of education than Trump had in governing, and who, like Trump, believes her money and Republican affiliation entitles her to govern where "angels fear to tread"..

Indeed, it may not be much of a stretch to view DeVos as Trump in drag.

In any event, Trump is NOT the Secretary of Education, and he is NOT going to expand two-four year vocation technical education, because that requires legislation, and legislation is what Congress does, NOT the President.

By promising to expand two-four year vocation technical education, Trump deceived voters that he had the authority to do so, when Trump knew, or should have known, he had no such authority, thereby fraudulently inducing voters to vote for him

Trump: <u>"I'm making two-four year college more affordable."</u>

Once again Trump is usurping the roll of Congress which has sole jurisdiction over funding, and over his Secretary of Education, who would have to take the lead in instigating, but not making, two-four year college more affordable.

By making this promise, Trump once again demonstrates his basic, but self-serving misunderstanding of the difference between a republic and a monarchy, of the separate and distinct roles of the three branches of government, the role of the President, "checks and balances," – a fundamental misunderstanding – more likely Trump's refusal to accept that reality of limits of power, all of which, should have counseled voters – a vote for Trump will be a vote to convert the Republic into a dictatorship of, by, and for, Donald J. ("J" for "Joke" – very bad joke) Trump.

Trump. <u>"We're (I'm) bringing education locally."</u>

We tried that before. It was called "separate but equal": and was determined to be unconstitutional in the 1954 Supreme Court case, *Brown v. Toledo Board of Education.*

Republicans and Conservatives keep trying to get control of public education – controlling the message – propaganda, without which there would no viable Republican Party and no Conservative take-over of America.

Do the math. How else can 10% of the population control 90%?

Time was when only the 10% got educated, usually by tutors paid to come into the homes of the wealthy and privileged. Kicking and screaming, the rich finally agreed to publicly fund schools for the rest of us, but public schools in America never received the same level of per capita funding as did prep schools for the rich, to wit, Phillips Andover, Phillips Exeter, and Groton. (Tuition at Phillips Andover is $48.850. Per pupil cost at Andover public schools is $25185.)

Not until 1852, was the first compulsory school attendance law passed. (Massachusetts). As expected, public schools in the South have always ranked at the bottom in whatever criteria is selected. (Nate Turner got Bible smart and look what happened.)

Conservative Republican poster boy, Ronnie Reagan, even tried to get rid of the Department of Education. Latter day Conservative zealots like Bush II and now Trump, use a double-barrel shotgun to kill public education, first irst, by under- funding public schools. Second, take public tax revenues to support religious schools, which, of course, violates the First Amendment prohibition against the establishment of religion, as does giving churches tax free property, but Conservatives use the Constitution and Bible only when it services their efforts to usurp control.

Then with public education convulsing in its death throes, Conservatives stick a knife in its back with school vouchers.

Trump's promise to do education "local" is a treacherous fraud perpetrated on the American voter in order to control the "message," as in "creationism."

Trump: <u>"I'm going to place a hiring freeze on all federal employees to reduce the workforce through attrition, except military, public safety, and public health."</u>

Five days after being sworn in, and before department Secretaries had been hired, or those hired had found their desks, and without considering the effect on federal employees, King Donald I orders a hiring freeze on non-military and non-security employees.

Why so presumptive Mr. Trump? Just letting everyone know you're in charge -- you get a "rush" controlling the lives of two million federal workers -- almost as much as another Narcissistic President enjoyed "frying" inmates on Texas's Death Row.

Ok. Trump seems to have the authority to do a hiring freeze, the lives of the 2 million federal employees so much collateral damage!

Trump did indeed impose a hiring freeze, so "yes" to treacherous power-mongering, but "no" to fraudulent inducement.

Trump: <u>"My requirement is for every new federal regulation, two existing regulations must be eliminated."</u>

"My requirement"! Trump really believes he IS the government!

He refuses to accept his temporary job as President as being to "execute" the Office in the best interests and benefits of ALL the people, but rather that the government is that authority which enables Trump to demand and command the people to cater to Donald's self-indulgent narcissism, and perks.

Who decides which two regulations get eliminated? Donald, of course. Who will stop Trump from dumping a truckload of bureaucratic regulations just to get rid of *Brown v. Board of Education,* or *Roe v. Wade?* No one, of course.

Would Republicans and Conservatives participate in such treachery? Didn't they just shoot the bird at the Constitution by refusing to vote on Obama's Supreme Court nominee on the chance a Republican would win and put one of their own on the Supreme Court?

Luckily, Presidents don't – can't – shouldn't -- make regulations. Congress does, therefore, Trump's promise to dump two regulations for every one adopted is a fanciful, unworkable, unmanageable and treacherous over-reach of presidential authority.

By promising to swap two existing regulations for each new regulation – a deal Trump knew, or should have known he has neither the right nor authority to make, Trump fraudulently induced voters to vote for him.

Trump:.”I'm going to issue a lifetime ban against senior executives and branch officials lobbying on behalf of a foreign government.”

I have to believe the President of the United States does not have the right and the authority to enforce a lifetime ban on anyone, so despite Trump's rare and apparent benign intent, it's still just another promise Trump should not have made and which can't be kept, therefore, making this promise a fraudulent inducement of voters to vote for him

Trump:.”I will defund Planned Parenthood because I'm pro-life.”

By uttering those eight words, Trump admits his allegiance and loyalty is to himself NOT to the government – not the people -- of the United States, that Trump is, in fact,, acting on behalf of Donald J. Trump, an entity other than, and foreign to, the United States – a traitorous act for which Trump must be tried, convicted, sentenced, and jailed as “Convict Donald.”

Trump: “I am looking to” (I'm going to) “appoint judges very much in the mold of

<u>Justice Scalia. I've actually picked 20 of them so</u>
<u>that people would see."</u>

Once again Trump demonstrates both a dangerous and treacherous ignorance of the Constitution, specifically its contract to provide **a fair and impartial judiciary for all citizens**. (To be sure, that promise has been broken more often than it has been fulfilled, but that must not be seen as a justification for Conservatives to shred the Constitution -- throw the law out with the lawbreakers.

"The most sacred of the duties of government is to do equal and impartial justice to all its citizens." Thomas Jefferson.

(Acknowledging we sin, prompts us to do less, not more sinning.)

Nixon, Reagan, Bushes I and II, knew they were violating the substance and intent of our Founding fathers like Jefferson by stacking the Supreme Court with Fundamentalist Conservative ideologues.

But given the choice of achieving a Conservative coup of America versus being true to the Constitution, Nixon, Reagan, Bush I and Bush II, via Rehnquist, Scalia, *et al*, rendered the Constitution just so much collateral damage on their way to making Conservative doxology the State's religion. (See John Dean's *Worse than Watergate*, where Dean describes how neo-Conservatives ignore, use, or abuse, (the 2nd Amendment), the Constitution depending on whether it defeats (2000 election of Dubya") or can be redacted (first 13 words of the 2nd Amendment) to suit their agenda.

Trump, on the other hand, cannot distinguish himself – his ego -- from the body politic, which, in his deluded *Weltanschauung,* is simply an extension of Donald's wants, needs, and delusional love of self.

But "yes," Trump can nominate who he pleases for the US Supreme Court, but "no" having sworn to "preserve, protect, and defend the Constitution," Trump cannot knowingly nominate someone who has professed his loyalty and allegiance to a Fundamentalist Conservative catechism, without incurring liability under both civil and criminal law, either one of which would be grounds for his removal.

Trump: <u>"We need to reform our mental health programs and institutions in this country."</u>

Amen, brother Donald, amen. Let's start with getting rid of the main cause of America's current epidemic of mental malaise – its *strum und drang* – its anxiety, depression, its sleepless nights, sense of shame, its fear of what its deluded President might do next – YOU!

Trump: <u>"I will withdraw from NAFTA."</u>

Go for it Donald. I didn't know NAFTA let individuals join. That said, I wouldn't be surprised if you're the only non-country member. After all, your boundless ego probably exceeds the mass of most countries.

On the unlikely chance Trump is speaking for America's interests and not his own, may I be so presumptuous as to suggest that the pulse of America be taken, assuming Americans know what NAFTA is and why WE joined in the first place, to be followed by a series of televised discussions/debates involving an equal number of authorities for and against NAFTA, before WE decide to stay or leave NAFTA. (It may be just me, but I've not lived under a tyrant/dictator before and I don't want to get used to it.)

For promising to withdraw from NAFTA as a show of kick-ass rebuke of all things Clinton and Obama, rather than a good-faith effort to assist the unemployed voter, Trump, invites the charge fraudulently inducing voter to vote for him.

.   **Trump**: "<u>I will withdraw from the Trans-Pacific Partnership.</u>"

Because, just as Bush II withdrew from Clinton's Kyoto Accords and purged all things Bill Clinton, Trump withdraws from the Trans-Pacific Partnership to purge all things Obama -- Bush II and Trump as male lions eating the cubs of the previous lion king.

But both Bush II and Trump, sacrifice the good of country on the altar of their own Narcissistic personalities, when, in fact, both are weak pretenders to the Presidency of the United States.

For promising to withdraw from the Trans-Pacific Partnership as a show of kick-ass rebuke of all things Obama, rather than a good-faith effort to assist the unemployed voter, Trump invites the charge fraudulently inducing voters to vote for him.

Trump: <u>"I will direct the Secretary of the Treasury to label China a currency manipulator,."</u>

That's the same kind of bellicose saber-rattling which the world finds repulsive in North Korea's Kim Jong-Un, and makes Trump seem to be cut from the same cloth.

Had Trump considered he is shooting himself in the foot in his efforts to later ask China to help reign in Kim Jong – Un?

Of course not. Once a bully always a bully.

The world needs two Narcissistic Personality Disorders playing "chicken" with nuclear missiles like it needs a worldwide attack by bacteria immune to all known antibiotics.

It's all a ruse of course. Trump is deceiving voters that he is this all-knowing- all-powerful, kick-ass, non-political, "outsider," Super-cop, who is going deport all the Mexican-illegal's who are stealing jobs from "real" Americans, build a wall to keep out the Mexicans who Trump alleges are bringing in drugs, using drugs, and raping our women, ban Muslims to prevent them from attacking us and taking over our country, undo all that that African-American President Obama did, falsely claiming Obamwasn't even born in America and never should have been allowed to run for President, repeal and replace Obamacare, send military weapons to local police, protect, defend, and support NRA, allow drilling, and mining in national parks, cut funding for school lunches, get rid of Common Core, reduce corporate taxes to below that of the average American wage-earner --- all part of Trump's Populist ploy to appear to be a friend of the working man, when in truth, Trump is exploiting that hypothetical worker so he can build a base of loyal followers – "Trump's Troops," who he can then count on to vote for him.

In truth, Trump is a Nixon "law & order,""Southern strategy" white supremacist, "segregation now, segregation "tamora' and segregation forever," George Wallace, a Reagan 'trickle-down, and a Dubya "fryem," closet Neo-Nazi, Conservative Republican.

For having deceived American voters (and pundits) that he is a "Populist"—like Hitler claiming to be an ERJ candidate (Equal Rights for Jews), Trump's con of mass deception represents fraud in the inducement and fraud of voters.

Trump: " <u>I will lift restrictions on the production of shale, oil, natural gas, and clean coal.</u>"

And may all the miners who die, or are disabled by brown lung disease, sue Donald Trump PERSONALLY, for depraved indifference and wrongful death.

This time, an evil Trump sacrifices the lives of coal miners in West Virginia and western Pennsylvania, by promising unregulated coal mining, which Trump knew, or should have known, would cause the death of more coal miners, and render more coal miner's families

fatherless and brother less, thereby indicting
Trump for the crimes of "depraved indifference,"
accessory to the deaths of unnamed coal miners,
fraud in the inducement and criminal fraud.

Trump; <u>"I will cancel billions in
payments to U.N. climate change programs and
use the money to fix America's water an
environmental infrastructure."</u>

It is impossible for Trump to act other
than in his own narcissistic interests. So, for
some perverse reason, probably because Obama
supported UN climate change funding, Trump
believes he can win the hearts, minds, and
admiration of his base by back-stabbing Obama,
taking on the Big Bad United Nations, and
reneging on the US's contractual financial
obligations to the UN, none of which Trump has
the power or authority to do anyway, because
Congress controls the purse strings.

Trump's grandiose delusion that he is the
all powerful, all knowing king/tyrant/ dictator
and unitary President, puts Americans at risk of
making enemies of our friends, and giving
comfort to our enemies.

We can stand aside as have the castrated
eunuch Republican males, excepting warrior
McCain, capitulate to Trump's bullying, or we
can take to the streets until Trump/Pence are
driven from the White House and the popular
vote winner of the election is installed as
President.

Meanwhile, Trump's promise "to cancel
billions in payments to U.N. climate change

programs," is the province of Congress, cannot be kept by Trump, and therefore is another instance of fraud in the inducement.

Trump: <u>"I will cancel every unconstitutional executive action, memorandum, and order issued by President Obama."</u>

Trump is as obsessed with desecrating Obama as Bush II was obsessed with defaming Bill Clinton,

Observe the extent to which Trump abuses and misuses his presidency in the service of his mental disorder -- the best interests of the American citizenry be damned!

Finally, having himself violated the Constitutional provision of three co-equal branches of government, and by willfully and maliciously "stacking" the Supreme Court with a known Conservative zealot, thereby showing no signs he has read, or cared to read, the Constitution of the United States, and since demonstrating a petulant, puerile, personal, and petty, antipathy toward President Obama, I, for one, will not trust Trump to decide which, if any, of President Obama's executive orders, or memorandums are "unconstitutional."

By abusing the Office of the President to induce racist voters to vote for him, Trump promises to violate his sworn oath to "preserve, protect, and defend the Constitution."

Trump: "<u>I will cancel all federal funding
to sanctuary cities,</u>:

O f course he will. To expect Trump
would do otherwise, is to lose sight of the fact
that arrogance, haughtiness, and an inability to
feel empathy for the needs and feeling of others
define Trump as a Narcissistic Personality
Disorder.

As funding is what Congress does, NOT
the President, and because Trump is again
making campaign promises not his to make, and
because he knew, or should have known better,
this promise rises to the level of fraud in the
inducement,thereby voiding his presidency

Trump : "<u>I will begin removing the more
than 2 million criminals; illegal immigrants from
the country.</u>"

In the grand tradition of Conservative
"kickass," fry'em,' "three strikes you're out,"
"law and order," politicians beginning with
Nixon, whose criminal acts would have
impeached him if he didn't resign and whose
Vice-President Agnew was jailed for tax evasion
, Conservatives have appealed to the worst
instincts--fear and hate -- to get elected.

Wait a minute. Who determined there are
"two million criminals"? Chronic liar and
Hitleresque propagandist Donald J. Trump? Of
course, who else?

Trump continues where Bush II left off.
Terrorists were Dubya's whipping boys;
immigrants from Mexico, Latin, and South

America and Muslims are Trumps. (The more tyrannical the leader, the more he pushes fear and hatred of an enemy. (If Dubya and Donald were not constantly having to keep up the appearance of superiority, they would not need to create dragons – mortal enemies to be slain – Dubya's Bill Clinton and Saddam Hussein – Donald's Obama and Kim Jong-Un.)

Trump gets the same "rush" hunting Mexicans trying to find a better life for themselves and their families as "Dubya did electrocuting mentally retarded and women inmates.

Still, Trump knew, or should have known, there were not "2 million migrant criminals who must be rounded up and deported," and the fraudulent information was stated to induce voters to vote for him.

Trump: "<u>I will cancel visas to foreign countries that won't take back criminal illegal immigrants.</u>"

"I", "I"."I" – not ever "The Government of the United States," and once or twice "we," as if Trump is deluded into believing that he is more than the country he has been temporarily – to end none too soon-- elected to represent. Indeed, in Trump's deranged mind, The United States Government, its 2 million employees, and the 327 million American residents, are in the service of Donald's narcissism – his every act of grandiosity, exaggerated claims of success, shameless lies, Mussolini-like braggadocio, and hourly acts of erratic behavior and irrational statements – all for sole purpose of grabbing the world's attention, in turn to deceive voters to vote for him.

Trump is not the President of the United States, in truth, the United States is subsumed under the personage of Donald J.Trump, When he refers to "I," he *de facto* declares," I am the Lord God and thou shall have no other Gods before me."

So, when he announces,"I will cancel visas to foreign countries that won't take back criminal illegal immigrants," he need not consider if he is counting "criminals" as those who enter the US with criminal records, or become criminalized in the United States, or what effect deporting will have on the arrestee's family..For example, will deporting the father force his family to go on welfare, or whether charging the "criminal" a fine is more cost-effective than the cost of deportation and supporting the family deportation leaves behind in the US.

.   A Trump as President of the United States, representing the best interests of all its citizens, would seek advice and counsel in addressing these and allied issues BEFORE issuing his *ex cathedra* decree.

A Trump representing only his self-interests, *uber alles*, the United States be damned, would announce,""I will cancel visas to foreign countries that won't take back criminal illegal immigrants, with total disregard for the leaders, or people, of the countries involved, all for the sole purpose to get elected.

If not fraud, then gross dereliction of

duty.

Trump: "<u>I will suspend immigration
from terror-prone regions where vetting cannot
safely occur.</u>"

It is impertinent to suggest to Herr
Donald that immigrants trying to avoid being
killed would be most in need to flee "terror-
prone regions,"
As an aside, the most pertinent lesson to
be gleaned from the fact of the Trump presidency
is that from that moment on, Americans must
begin vetting its presidential candidates as to
psychological and psychiatric illness and
disorders, with specific focus on the Narcissistic
Personality Disorder, as two Narcissistic
Personality Disorders have become Presidents in
just the past 16 years, with disastrous results –
two fraudulent wars in Afghanistan and Iraq
resulting in the death of some 7,000 American
soldiers, as many as a MILLION civilians killed
or displaced, Armageddon in the Middle East,
and a Not-so Great Depression.
We are left with the untenable position
that his Holiness Donald will decide which
regions are "terror-prone," when Trump knew, or
should have known, that decision is not his to
make, meaning it is another fraudulent attempt to
induce voters to vote for him.

Trump: "<u>I will impose "extreme
vetting," on all people coming into our country.</u>"

More fantasy of power and self-importance, in which he presumes the prior vetting process, which has prevented foreign terrorist attacks since 9/11 is inferior to his, and being too arrogant and too almighty to offer a definition of "extreme vetting," Trump anoints himself cop, prosecutor, judge and jury.

Why not? Because his grandiose delusion of being the final word entitles him to rule as infallible as the Pope.

Trump has trashed government as we knew it since 1781, basically pulling off a one man coup/, and replacing it with Dictator,/Tyrant/King, aka Donald Trump.

His promise to impose extreme vetting, was not his to make, and was done to deceive voters he had powers he didn't have, making the promise fraudulent on its face.'

Trump: "<u>I will establish a 2-year mandatory minimum federal prison sentence for illegally re-entering the US. after previous deportation.</u>"

More "kick-ass," Old Testament rhetoric to win the admiration of his pre-Christ "take no prisoners," evangelical base.

It would seem the nomination of Conservative Scalia-wannabe Gorsuch was superfluous with Judge Trump already occupying that seat by proxy,

Actually, Trump doesn't get to determine the federal prison sentences of anyone. The Bureau of Prisons or the Attorney General's Justice Department may ask – recommend Congress pass laws regarding prison sentences, but Trump knew, or should have known, his "law and order" campaign promise noted above was an attempt to fraudulently induce voters to vote for him.

Trump; <u>"I will establish a 5-year mandatory minimum sentence for illegally re-entering for those with felony convictions or multiple misdemeanors convictions."</u>

Where is it written the President of the United States writes laws? Oh, but Sir Donald is not just the President of the United States, but much more – the *de facto* ruler of the Executive, Legislative, and Judicial branches of government – a pre- 1215 Magna Carter, king.

Trump makes Nixon's "Imperial Presidency and Dubya's Diabolical Presidency seem almost Athenian democratic.

Trump's campaign promise willfully and treacherously misleads naive voters into believing he has governmental power he does not have, thereby fraudulently inducing voters to vote for him

Trump<u>. "1 will reform rules to ensure open jobs are first offered to American workers."</u>

So far, Trump has eliminated the need for a cabinet,. Congress, the Departments of State, Education, Justice, the Supreme Court, and Homeland Security, so why not Labor?

By the time Donald has completed his grandiose list of campaign promises, he will have reduced the need of federal employees from two million to one – Himself.

Finally, Trump knew, or should have known, the President does not write laws and rules, and therefore he could not promise to "reform rules." making this a promise to fraudulently induce voters to vote for him.

Trump: "<u>I will establish screening of immigrants to ensure they support our people and our values</u>"

Too grandiose even by Trump's deluded standards, too arrogant, and too obvious a ploy to win the Trump vote.

In his rush to receive a standing ovation from the low end of his base for his shameless jingoism and neo-Nazi racism, Trump deludes himself that telling employees on his TV show, "You're fired, "qualifies Donald to research, develop, and 'establish" a screening protocol "to ensure that immigrants first "support our people and our values,"

Tell us Mr. Trump, how is an immigrant, by definition, able to "support' an unknown people he/she may only know via TV and propaganda. Two, an immigrant cannot be expected to "support our values," when 65 % of Americans polled, don't support their President and his values?

More fraudulent posturing by Trump as a "hard-ass" in order to induce – deceive voters to vote for him.

Trump: "<u>I will reform visa rules to</u>

ensure penalties for over-staying."

Build walls, hunt migrants as if they were coyotes, deport parents so as to leave children without a mother or father, hire more border patrol, more police, more guards, more air port screeners – Trump's solution to his paranoia is a police state with Trump as the Super Cop -- the Terminator – crossing the line from "lacking empathy" to being a sadist who enjoys inflicting pain on others – the employer who gets off telling his employees, "You're fired."
Trump's promise to reform rules is not his promise to make, rendering his promise fraud in the inducement to get voters to vote Trump.

Trump: "I will create a task force on violent crime."

Ok, but re-word your promise to say, "The Executive Branch will work with all the appropriate agency leaders in creating a task force to look into the causes and remedies of violent crime in America.
See. It's not that difficult, AND you avoid being charged with defrauding voters.

Trump: "I will increase funding for programs that train and assist local police."

There are those who naively presumed that Trump's lack of political experience meant he is "no politician."
Fools fooled. Trump beat slick politicians Rubio, Cruz,, Jeb Bush, Chris

Christie, Mike Huckabee, Rand Paul, and Rick
Santorum by being the better politician – more
ruthless. more bullying and the better liar to be
sure, but always the better politician.

Trump also knew, as did Goebbels,
Nixon, Reagan, Karl Rove, and Bush II, that the
masses are best manipulated by slogans, bumper
stickers, one-liners, and lies repeated often
enough until the masses believe them to be true.

Trump, who would make Josef Goebbels
flinch, repeated the words "convict' and
"Hillary:" so often that by the time Trump's
devotees entered the voting booth, they were
convinced Hillary should have been in jail by
now. (Goebbels instructed us that, "A lie told
once remains a lie, but a lie told a thousand time
becomes the truth." Trump practiced what
Goebbels' preached.

Politician Trump also understood that his
flock thinks "black or white," "good or bad,"
"right or wrong," meaning Nixon's, Reagan's,
and Bush II's "law and order," "tough on crime'
and pro-police state rhetoric would draw the
lower-end masses to his rallies like flies to
dinosaur dung,

Meanwhile Trump's promise to fund
police-training programs is as fatally flawed as
his other promises, to wit, Congress does the
funding , and any promises in that regard rest
with the Legislative branch , not the Executive
branch. Deceiving the voters otherwise is a
fraudulent inducement to vote from Trump.

Trump: "I will increase resources for
federal law enforcement agencies and federal

<u>prosecutors to dismantle criminal gangs, and
put violent offenders behind bars."</u>

In politics, fear moves voters more than
any other emotion – the "Red Scare" of the
1920'- 1980's, the Nate Turner scare in the
South before there was a Nate Turner, the
Terrorist scare beginning in the US with the 9/11
bombing, the current Muslim scare, and the Kim
Jong-Un/Donald Trump scare beginning on
August 8, 2017.

So far the evidence is clear and
compelling to all those with IQ's over 85, not
being identified as one of Trump's crazies –
"deplorables," and not sporting a personality
disorder, or paranoid schizophrenia diagnosis, is
that the 50 year history of the Conservative
solution to crime is building more prisons and
longer arbitrary prison sentences, the solution to
the drug problem is more cops and more prisons,
the solution to gun killings is more guns, and the
solution to terrorism is a police state, has been
proven wrong on all counts.

So, now, too arrogant and too glutted
with grandiose illusions of omniscience, Donald
J. Trump offers, inter-country border walls, more
border patrol, more guards, more police, and
more prisons, begging the question: Is Trump
proposing to make American great again by
going back to 50 years of failed Conservative
programs and policies?

If Trump's promise to increase sources
for police involves money, Congress is privy to
such promises NOT Trump.

More Trump fraud in the Inducement and

reason to remove him from the presidency.

Trump: "<u>I'm going to expand our military investment.</u>"

Only if Trump puts his personal funds into the Pentagon which I'm certain is illegal. Any expansion of the "military investment" will occur if Congress says it will, and Congress, not Trump, will determine the amount of the investment..

Another fraudulent Trump promise to induce voters to vote for Trump.

Trump: "<u>I will provide veterans with the ability to receive public VA treatment or private doctor of veteran's choice.</u>"

Trump suffers from delusions of grandeur, in, that he now owns the Federal Government, having bought it on January 20th, 2017, and is thereby entitled to do with it as he would with any other company or property he owns..

Three problemswe American citizens must soon face: (1) How much damage to America's body politic will Trump inflict as the direct result of his narcissistic self-indulgences and excesses? (2) Donald's delusion that he is superior, divined to rule and conquer, achieve unlimited success, and entitled to the world's highest rewards and admiration, is on a collision course with the humbling reality of being the President, not the owner, of the United States. (3) What price will Americans pay when Donald is publically forced to face failure he can't blame on others? (Trump has already fired his policy advisor Sam Nunberg, transition team member, Chris Christie, acting Attorney General Sally Yates, US Attorney Bharara, Mike Flynn, his National Security Adviser, FBI Director James Comey, White House Chief of Staff Reince Priebus (forced to resign), Press Secretary Spicer, Communications Director Anthony Sccaramucci, Michael Short (resigned) and Angela Reid ,Chief White House usher from Obama's presidency, America's Trotsky, aka Steve Bannon, Health and Human Services Secretary Tom Price, threatened to fire Attorney General Sessions, but with each instance of blaming others, as Narcissistic Personalities must do because they are deluded as to their infallibility, Trump reveals the extent of his mental illness and his inability to " faithfully execute the Office of President of the United States.)

Trump leads his lawless legions in Civil War II? Trump buys the White House, forecloses on the Government, and sets up his alternative government in Mar-a-Lago? Or worse: Trump changes his hair color?

Trump can blame the media, 3 million "illegal voters," the Democrats, an FBI "witchunt," "leaks", "fake' news" an inept Mitch McConnell – Mitch had been inept way before Trump thought about running – House Speaker "Chameleon" Ryan, the Republicans, Hillary, Bill, Obama, but with each ranting Tweet, Donald J, Trump, exposés himself as a pathetic mental case, a "sicko" and a fraud.

Trump: "<u>I will create at least 10 million jobs in the first term.</u>"

No one – not the Pope, not Donald the First, and not Bill Gates, "creates" jobs, Companies hire workers and staff because they predict they will make more money from the labor than they would if they didn't hire them.

Furthermore, an increase in jobs may be due to the continuing trend of economic recovery initiated by the Democratic Obama Administration to dig us out of the depression caused by Republican President Bush II"s UNREGULATED mortgage banking companies..

Trump taking credit for the current Stock Market obscenity, like taking credit for the Gorbush nomination, is analogous to the Republicans taking credit for Clarence Thomas. In all three instances, the outcome is cause of chagrin.

Both the giddy Stock Market and job increases are collateral damage to Trump's promise to repeat Dubya's mistake of across the board deregulation – unregulation in Dubya's case.

Capitalists now have one of their own – albeit a monstrous example – on the throne of Capitalism's empire, who promises to "make America great again" – again meaning a return to the unregulated "trickle-down" economic busts of Reagan and Bush II.

So, we have another meltdown: The mortgage bankers who caused the last meltdown received two taxpayer bailouts of $700 BILLION each,, and other than a bothersome inconvenience, are doing better now than before.

Yes, but millions of American homebuyers were foreclosed by the same mortgage bankers and put out in the street. About the same number lost their jobs.

How did the capitalists justify this evil and predatory pillage of American's home and loss of jobs: "Law of the jungle – "survival of the fittest' – "creationists" conveniently converted to Darwinism.

And what happened to those millions rendered homeless and jobless by Republican President George Dubya Bush's policy of unregulated businesses?

Eight years later, they swear their undying and inexorable allegiance to Conservative Republican Neo-Nazi Nationalist Donald J. Trump, promising to undo all of Democrat President Obama's regulations put in place to prevent another Republican-engineered meltdown.

Go figure, or read. *Trump's Troops Revolt Against Republican Party's Betrayal,* R.G. Coleman, Ph.D. Uncommon Sense Publications, 2017, Amazon.)

Meanwhile, Trump's outrageous Big Lie promise that he will create 10 million jobs, is a cruel and evil exploitation of the unemployed who Trump fraudulently induces to vote for him.

Trump: <u>"I will give a middle-class family with two children a 35% tax cut."</u>

Our politicians and Federal employees have surrendered the Government of the United States to a Narcissistic Personality so ignorant, so arrogant, and so deluded that he believes he is the sole proprietor of said Government entitled to do as he wishes, and who wishes only to make said Government a playground on which he exercises his narcissism.

Dubya also promised tax cuts -- $400. for the average American household and MILLONS to America's millionaires.

Trump's proposal to reduce corporate taxes from 39% to 15%, which means corporate America will pay less than the average middle-class wage earner, making Trump's tax package a plagiarized version of Dubya's tax scheme with the same result -- A pittance for the middle class and millions for the millionaires.

Trump's tax cuts is a self-serving conflict of interest fraud and hoax – Big Lie – to fraudulently induce voters to vote for him.

Trump:" <u>I will reduce the number of tax brackets from seven to three and likewise greatly simplify tax forms.</u>"

No, Donald you won't do any of the above for three reasons. First, Congress, not you as President, drafts and votes up or down on tax laws. Second, because you stand to gain millions from your so- called "tax reform, you must face charges of "conflict of interest' if you try to influence federal tax laws. Third, for having refused to release your tax returns over the protest of American citizens and US Senators, you waive your right to influence tax laws, making your promise to reduce tax brackets more fraud in the inducement -- deceiving voters you have jurisdiction over tax laws, which you do not..

Trump: <u>"I will lower the business tax rate from 35% to 15%"</u>

Not unless you want to be impeached for conflict of interests, and/or strung up by your ankles by an angry mob like your mentor Mussolini.

CONGRESS, NOT THE PRESIDENT WRITES AND PASSES TAX LAWS.

By misrepresenting to the voters that Trump drafts and passes tax legislation Trump fraudulently induced voters to vote for him!

Trump<u>: "I will grow the economy 4% a year."</u>

More fraud in the inducement. Trump knew or should have known that no one person "grows" the economy.

And while, Trump deludes himself that he alone deserves the credit for low employment and stock market gains, rather than giving credit to Obama's eight years of recovery from Dubya's Depression, recent Stock Market highs may be the indirect result of businessman Trump's signaling his fellow capitalists that the good (bad for non-capitalists) old days are back again – obscene low corporate taxes, and a deregulated economy. (Apparently Trump's "time" when

America was great occurred 2000- 2007,) during Dubya's debauched presidency – two illegal wars still being fought and depression.

Trump: <u>"I will establish tariffs to discourage companies from laying off their workers in order to relocate in other countries and shift their products back to the U.S. tax-free."</u>

No you won't. Butt out. Not in your job description.

Article I, Section 7 – "The Origination Clause" of the Constitution of the United States reads "All Bills for raising Revenue shall originate in the House of Representatives, but the Senate may propose or concur with Amendments as on other Bills/."

Tariffs were and still are considered "bills to raise revenue," and in fact, prior to passage of the 16th Amendment – the income tax Amendment of 1913, tariffs were a main source of revenue for operating the Federal government.

Tariffs are a source of revenue, *ipso facto,* Congress, NOT the president "establishes tariffs."

Deceiving voters by promising them he will "establish tariffs, he knew, or should have known, are the purview of Congress, Trump incurs liability for fraudulently inducing voters to vote for him

Trump: <u>"I will leverage public-private partnerships and private investments through tax</u>

incentives to spur $1trillion in infrastructure
investment over 10 years."

Trump acts as if there were no Congress,
or that he, as President of the United States, can
usurp the role of the House of Representatives
and Senate whenever he wishes to do so. And
while such behavior confirms Donald's diagnosis
as a Narcissistic Personality Disorder, such
confirmation is redundant and insignificant in
the context of Trump's daily assaults on the
Constitution of the United States, already tattered
by 50 years of Neo-Conservatives imposing their
 theocratic capitalism to "make America great
again."
By deceiving voters that he has the power
and authority to implement his grandiose scheme
of "leveraging partnerships' and "private
investments," while managing "tax incentives to
spur $1 trillion for infrastructure,' Trump incurs
liability for having fraudulently induced voters to
vote for him.

Trump: "I will redirect education money
to give parents the right to send their kid to the
public, private charter, magnet, religious, or
home school of their choice."

Right! The Right Religious Wrongs – aka
" State's Righters," have been treacherously
trying to eviscerate public education – regain
control of the message – get back to
proselytizing children, which was. and is, the
sole purpose of all so-called "religious schools
and colleges, to wit, the first "public" schools in

America were *de facto* religious schools where Protestant theology dominated the curriculum, and in some parts of rural America, it still does – "creationism" nonsense being but one recent example.

By 1918, every state required children to at least complete elementary school, and by the 1930's, children were being taught a more diverse and secular curriculum – Latin and religion were out, civics and PE were in.

Following the 1954 Supreme Court decision of *Brown v.. Topeka Board of Education,* America's schools were ordered to integrate, forcing children to right the segregation/racism wrongs of their parents,

Suddenly, but predictably, church schools sprouted in the south like forgotten relatives at a reading of the Will -- a willful, illicit, and malicious attempt to sabotage integration, in turn, pitting the liberal, mostly northern, proponents of integration, against the Conservative, mostly southern proponents of segregation -- "Conservative "State's Righterss" versus the Liberal Big Bad Federal Government, in all matters of education.

As recently as 1982, Conservative Republican Reagan tried to get rid of the U.S. Department of Education. Bush II tried to do the same with vouchers, Trump tries both –vouchers and DeVos.

Texas Conservative President Bush II violated the intent and spirit of the US Supreme Court in *Brown,* violated the First Amendment prohibition against Federal support of religion, and the founding principle of separation of church and state, by illegally federally funding church school vouchers, and "faith-based" programs.

But what politician, during these times of the Conservative pogrom of all non-Conservatives, dares commit political suicide by refusing to give unto the Christian God, that which is lawfully Caesar's?

Trump, a neo-Conservative, closet neo-Nazi zealot, wearing the cloak of a "Populist" to appeal more broadly – but by deed and word, a true-Anti-Christ, now promises voters he "will redirect education money to give parents the right to send their kid to the public, private charter, magnet, religious, or home school of their choice."

"Shooting the bird" at the US Supreme Court in *Brown* by *de facto* resegregating public schools by race and income, announcing his intention to violate the First Amendment of Constitution prohibiting the "establishment" (financially supporting) of religion," and that he will violate the Blaine Amendment, which, in 34 states, prohibits using public funds to support parochial schools, Trump is not only fraudulently inducing voters to vote for him, but is soliciting their participation in a scheme to violate the Constitution – the same Consyitution Trump sore to "preserve, protect,an defend" – an seditios act warranting Trump's removal.

Trump: <u>"I will allow Americans to deduct child and elder care from their taxes."</u>
`

No you won't. Congress alone writes and passes tax laws. Besides, you waived your right – actually, you have no right to insert yourself into any and all considerations, discussions, and votes regarding income tax laws, first because such actions are to be taken by Congress, not you, second, you would be inviting a charge of "conflict of interest, and third, the public, already angered that you snuck in the back door of the White House with a key provided by the Electoral College, is likely to come looking for you, if you insert yourself into the income tax debate without revealing your own income tax files.

By promising voters that he has the power and authority over tax laws, he knew, or should have known he didn't, Trump incurs liability for the charge of fraud in the inducement

Trump : <u>"I will create tax-free dependent care savings accounts for young and elderly dependents.</u>"

Once again, only Congress can write and pass tax laws.

For promising voters, not Trump's to make and therefore promise, Trump knew, or should have known he couldn't keep, Trump is liable to his voters for fraud in the inducement.

Trump: <u>"I will fully repeal and replace Obamacare.</u>"

Big Lie. Only Congress can repeal and replace the Affordable Health Care Act, which

Republicans have been trying to subvert and destroy ever since it became law on March 23,2010, the health interests of the people be damned!

For the next seven years, Republicans have made repeal and replacement of the renamed Obamacare their *raison d'être* – their *cause célèbre* – their sink or swim election slogan, regardless of the health protection and benefits to the 90%.

Trump made trashing Obamacare personal – a Narcissistic Personality Disorder consumed with envy – obsessed with replacing the former Number One – President Obama, with himself -- the health and welfare of millions of Americans – millions of his base – as just so much collateral damage. (It is noteworthy that with each successive Congressional failure to repeal and replace Obamacare, Trump decreased his involvement

Why Trump's retreat from the battle he promised to win? Narcissistic Personalities never lose, or at least refuse to accept responsibility for a loss or defeat. So, with each defeat to repeal and replace Obamacare, Trump inched further and further from the fray, poised to blame McConnell, but not so distant as to be unable to take the credit for the win.

Recall Trump is in denial – he didn't lose the popular vote by nearly three million -- those three million votes were "illegal," with no evidence of course for his claim, and defends his delusion by proposing a national voter-fraud investigation – itself a fraud – which will prove Hillary won only because three million votes for her were illegal.

Similarly, Trump didn't fail to keep his campaign promise to repeal and replace Obamacare; Senate majority leader Mitch McConnell failed to do his job.

No wonder Trump is envious of Obama; Trump is a callous, arrogant, ignorant, petty, merciless, ruthless, self-obsessed, cruel, and vindictive thug, who cares only for, and about, himself, with his immediate goal being the instant attention and admiration of all -- admiration to which he deludes himself he is entitled. .

The other reality is that Obama is intelligent, conscientious, sensitive, thoughtful, generous in h\is empathy and concern for others, whose warn, infectious, genuine smile reminds some of us of another beloved President and first Lady Michelle -- John Kennedy. and "Jacky". (On a personal note, I felt as privileged to be alive during Obama's presidency as I now feel ashamed to live during Trump's.)

There was never any doubt that Obama was acting in the best interests of all Americans, as he judged those interests by his deliberate and deep analysis and counsel, all the while, confronted by Republican's putting Party over Country, brazenly denouncing every rule, every regulation, or program offered or supported by President Obama.   Case in point: Republican Senate leader, Mitch McConnell/ too ignorant, too boorish, and too pedestrian to realize he was shamelessly abusing and misusing his role as US Senator to make certain "Obama becomes a one-term President."

One need only observe the difference between how Obama relates to his wife, Michelle – equal partner with equal respect and mutual love, versus Trump and Melania, who Trump parades as his trophy as if to show the world, "Look at the prize I won at the State fair!"

.   That Trump would be envious of Obama according to Criterion # 8 for a finding of Narcissistic Personality Disorder may be clinically reassuring, but when Trump's envy of Obama becomes the cause of Trump's national policy decisions --- his obsession to overturn, trash, repeal, and replace all things Obama, despite the benefits to Americans, **gives cause for Trump's removal from the office as President of the United States for felonious failure to faithfully execute the Office of President of the United States for ALL Americans.**

That Trump would promise voters," I will fully repeal and replace Obamacare,' after observing Congressional; Republicans trying for seven years to do just that, Trump had to know repeal and replace was the job of Congress, NOT the president. Yet he still deceived the voters, that he would do the job, not his to do, thereby fraudulently inducing voters to vote for him, and in the process voiding his presidency as having been obtained by fraud.

<u>Trump</u>: <u>"I will enact new ethics reforms to reduce corrupting influence of special interests."</u>

To paraphrase Johnny Carson, expecting Trump to enact new ethics reforms "would be like taking navigation lessons from the Captain of the Titanic."

WHEREAS, Trump's fraudulent campaign promises demonstrate a basic ignorance of, or arrogant refusal to accept, the fundamental working of the government of the United States – Its three co-equal branches -- Executive, Legislative, and Judicial -- that each branch has a distinct quasi-independent function and limited jurisdiction, and the role of the President is that of manager, not a player, with the Constitution as playbook and script for rules of governance. **WHEREAS**, Trump is 71, a college graduate. and contrary to his fraudulent representations to the public that, "I'm no politician," Trump's been in politics for 30 years, spending a reported $100,000 running full-page political "feeler" ads in 1987, being a third party candidate in 2000, considered running for president in 1988, 2000, 2004, and 2012, and for Governor of New York in 2006 and 2014. In March 2011, Trump was the leading contender for the Republican nomination for President. It was at that same time that Trump began his "birther" campaign – a slanderous, fraudulent, racist and evil attack on President Obama, falsely claiming, with NO evidence, that President Obama was born in Kenya, and therefore, ineligible to be President. (The fact of the "birther" slander and defamation should have killed Trump as a legitimate candidate for public office, thus sparing us the tragedy of his presidency.) Rather than being a non-politician, inexperienced in the corrupt and unseemly ways of Washington, Trump was as sullied, depraved, and conniving as the most seasoned, wicked, Washington wastrel. Trump knew how government and politicians worked, and **WHEREAS**, having ruled out ignorance and innocence as excuses for Trump's wanton disregard for the rules for engaging voters, we must presume that Trump deliberately made the above reported false, deceptive, misleading promises to voters as to what Trump had the power, authority, and Constitutional right to promise, thereby committing multiple acts of fraud in the inducement to persuade voters to vote for him.

To prevail in an action for fraud and fraud in the inducement against Trump, it must be shown that: (1) Trump made the fraudulent statements – he did, (2) the statements were false – they were, (3) Trump knew they were false, or made "recklessly without knowledge of its truth – he did both, (4) voters voted based on Trump's fraudulent statements – they did, and (5) we suffered injury and damages as the direct result of Trump becoming President – we did.

For example, we have lost trust and confidence in the Office of President, we suffer the loss of leadership of our Country, in turn, making us feel vulnerable from attacks at home and abroad. We feel betrayed by our government. We feel victims of our government rather than protected by it, and we are threatened by Trump's daily assaults on our Constitution – the very essence of our history and who we are as a people – our rights and protections.

We witness President Trump insulting and demeaning our allies, thereby making our friends our enemies, and giving comfort to our enemies. We squirm with every lie he tells and ashamed of his arrogance and bad manners on the world's stage. We become alarmed when he announces his support for white supremacists, neo-Nazis, neo-nationalists, and para-military groups – all promoting the overthrow of the Government of the United States, thereby revealing Donald Trump's true identity and loyalties, in turn, forcing us to the inexorable conclusion that our President is an enemy of the State

With Republicans in control of the House of Representative, the Senate, and the presidency, and with Conservative Republicans in control of the Republican Party, Congress, the White House, and the Supreme Court, unless Trump is caught in the act of humping the Statue of Liberty, Republicans, who historically put Party "values" over Country, will block any and every attempt to impeach Trump.

The other reality is that we have yet to save ourselves. from the Conservative Republican, depraved presidency of Dubya – his two fraudulent and unwinnable wars in Afghanistan and Iraq and his not-so-great "trickle-down," depression caused by UNREGULATED banks and mortgage companies -- America cannot and will not survive four years of Conservative Republican Trump's presidency, already more depraved, and promising more DEREGULATION, more "trickle-down" economics, and more wars!!

The third reality is that we have become a police state – (My small town very local Social Security Office has an armed cop inside the front door! I go to the local flea market and one of the vendors wears a damn gun!)

Our First Amendment right to peacefully assemble died on May 4, 1970, when, during their right to peacefully assemble four unarmed Kent State students were shot and killed by Ohio State National Guardsmen

Fast forward nearly 50 years -- Trump rescinds President Obama's order that the military stop providing military weapons and equipment to local police in an effort to reduce the appearance of a police state at the local level.

With impeachment unlikely, even if Prosecutor Robert Mueller uncovers "high crimes and misdemeanors, due to a hostile Conservative Republican Congress and a hostile Conservative Reoublican US Supreme Court, which threw the 2000 election to seat one of their own in the White House, and considering the increased odds of being shot and killed by a Trump supporter, or the police, while exercising our right to demand that Trump demonstrate his patriotism by resigning – taking Pence with him, and convinced the Republic will not survive four years of Trump's presidency, what's a patriot to do?

Consider this; "Fraud vitiates everything, a judgment equally with a contract," *US v. Throckmorton,* 98 U.S. 61 (1878).

"Fraud destroys the validity of everything into which it enters," *Nuddv. Burrows*, 91 U.S.436

"Fraud vitiates everything," *Biyce v. Grundy.* 3 Pet. 210.

"Out of fraud, no action arises; **fraud never gives a right of action.** No court will lend its aid to a man who founds his cause of action upon an immoral or illegal act," Black's law Dictionary, Fifth Edition, Page 509.

"We have no officers in this government from the President down to the most subordinate agent, who does not hold office under the law with prescribes duties and limited authority," *Pierce v. United States,* 7 Wall. (74 U.S.) 666-677..

Therefore, Donald J. Trump's contract with us, having been fraudulently obtained, must be "vitiated" – vacated -- as a matter of law, meaning, Trump was never President, so all Executive Orders, Laws, Bills, Initiatives, Rules and Appointments made by Trump must be voided, and the person who finished second in the election of 2016, shall be declared the winner and President of the United States.

<u>Count Two</u>

<u>Trump's Narcissistic Personality Disorder Renders Him Unable to Fulfill His Contract as President of the United States</u>

We will show that Donald J. Trump suffers from a mental disorder called "Narcissistic Personality Disorder", so pervasive and so debilitating as to render Trump unfit and unable to "faithfully execute the Office of President of the United States".

Named for Narcissus who, according to Greek mythology, when stopping by a pool, became so infatuated with his own reflection, that he fell in love with himself.

Freud described such persons as having a grossly distorted – deluded -- sense of self - importance, having delusions of greatness unsupported by reality, believes he is special, and needs to be admired accordingly.

The Narcissistic Personality grossly over-estimates his ability. For example, an untrained, inexperienced, and unqualified Trump is so deluded he believes he is entitled to be President of the United States

A Narcissistic Personality exaggerates his accomplishments with similar generosity, For example, Trump declares his presidency as the best the world has ever known."" (Recall Mussolini's pursed and protruding lips, his chin held high to highlight his hubris just as Trump does.)   The Narcissistic Personality glows with a sense of entitlement – his divined right accruing from his superior status. As all others are inferior to him, he sees his underlings as exploitable – to be used in service of his self-indulged narcissism as Trump is to his base.

A Narcissistic Personality is incapable of empathy – Trump's callous and merciless deporting of mothers and fathers leaving their children born in the United States parentless -- and is envious, suspicious, and dismissiveness of rivals who threaten his self-imposed position as Number One. – Trump slandering Hillary as "Killer Hillary" and his compulsion to repeal and replace Obamacare by whatever means necessary, without regard to the harm repeal and replace will have on others.

Delusions of grandeur cannot co-exist with ever being wrong, so any mistakes are the fault of others – Trump blaming staff leaks for his inept and dysfunctional governance.

A Narcissistic Personality never loses -- Trump didn't lose the popular vote by nearly three million votes, three million voters voted for Hillary illegally/

The singular act of Donald J. Trump, with no experience, no training, and no qualifications, would delude himself that he is entitled to become the President of the United States –that act alone defines Trump as a Narcissistic Personality Disorder

The *Diagnostic and Statistical Manual of Mental Disorders* (DSM –IV and V) ,which represents the consensus of America's psychiatrists and psychologists for diagnosing mental disorders, defines a Narcissistic Personality Disorder as, "A pervasive pattern of grandiosity (in fantasy or behavior), a need for admiration, and a lack of empathy, beginning by early adulthood and present in a variety of contexts. as indicated by five (or more) of the following criteria:

1.   A Narcissistic Personality Disorder manifests "a grandiose sense of self importance, for example, exaggerates achievements and talents, expects to be recognized as superior without commensurate achievement,"

In acts of grandiose delusions of self-importance, Trump reneged on his oath to "faithfully execute the Office of President of the United States and to "protect, preserve, and defend the Constitution," by: (a) Compromising our external and internal security and the integrity of our election by granting "most favored nation" status to Mr. Putin. (b) Abusing his authority, to wit, Trump loosed a daily deluge of Executive Orders to personally denigrate, defame, and disgrace Obama and his Administration, with no thought as to the benefit Obama's programs and regulations had on the American people. (c) Imposing his will, wants, and whims on Americans; with no concern as to what Americans; needed and wanted. For example, Trump installed a Draconian dragnet to indiscriminately deport immigrants, with no concern for the effect his mass deportations would have on children and families. (d) Violating the Constitution's promise of a "fair and impartial judiciary" by nominating Neil Gorsuch, for the very reason Gorsuch is an unfair and partial Conservative fundamentalist in the Scalia mold. (e) Inciting Civil War II, by turning his "base" of "deplorables." -- Neo-Nazis, White--Supremacists and KKK'ers, into a force, which, under Trump's command, promises to take over the Government of the United States and, (f) Self-.indulging in a war of words with equally narcissistic self-indulgent Kim Jung-Un, all the while being insouciant to the serious threat Trump's words have on the security of the citizens of the United States he claims to be protecting. with his "wall," his deportations, and Muslim bans.

2.   A Narcissistic Personality Disorder is "preoccupied with fantasies of unlimited success, power, brilliance, beauty or ideal love."

Trump's narcissistic fantasy of unlimited fame and success – "I'll be the greatest jobs President God ever made," "I will make America great again," "I will fully repeal and replace Obamacare." "I will build a wall along the Mexican border and make Mexico pay for it," "I'm the only one who knows how to build cities," and "I'll create 10 million jobs,"" enabled Trump to convince himself he should be President of the United States when, in reality, he is untrained, inexperienced, and unqualified, thereby precluding him from faithfully executing the Office of President of the United States, and preserving, protecting and defending the Constitution of the United States, in turn, placing Americans at severe risk of a government functioning at the behest of a deranged despot and contrary to the interests of the majority of Americans.

3.   A Narcissistic Personality Disorder "believes that he is special and unique and

can only be understood by, or should associate with, other special or high-status people or institutions,"

Trump nominated Conservative zealot and Scalia wannabe Gorsuch to the US Supreme Court, knowing: (a) Republicans had violated the rules by refusing to consider Obama's nominee. (b) By making the nomination of Gorsuch :personal and "in-your-face," Trump alienated Democrats, Independents, and Hillary//Obama/Sanders voters so that a Congress once divided became a Congress re-divided into war against Trump. (c) Rehnquist/Scalia & Roberts' extreme conservatism had broken the Constitution's promise of a fair and impartial judiciary. (d) Trump knew, should have known, and/or didn't care, that a continuation of a Conservative controlled Supreme Court, predicted further and irreversible shredding of the Constitution 'trickling down' from the Supreme Court to local district and circuit courts. (e) Trump's "personal" nomination" of Gorsuch violated the intent and spirit of the Constitution's commitment to fundamental fairness and the public's expectation of "equal protection under the laws' guaranteed by the Constitution Trump swore to preserve, protect and defend./

4.　　A Narcissistic Personality Disorder, "requires excessive admiration,"

Trump's rallies particularly those AFTER he has been elected, his vindictive and self-indulgent Executive Orders, daily photo-ops, tweets, and self-congratulatory policy statements are staged performances to feed Trump's narcissism, and as such, are self-serving, rather than, and often contrary to, the interests of the United States and its citizens.

Trump's loyalty and allegiance is to himself as a Narcissistic Personality -- a foreign, different, an alien entity other than the United States – "giving :aid and "comfort' to his narcissism at the expense of the Government of the United State thereby inviting a charge of "treason" against Trump no less damaging than secretly giving Russia "most favored status."

5. A Narcissistic Personality Disorder "has a sense of entitlement – unreasonable expectations of especially favorable treatment or automatic compliance with his or her expectations."

Believing he is entitled, and expecting automatic compliance, Trump orders the President of Mexico to pay for the wall Trump has promised his base he will build without first securing concurrence from the President of Mexico to build and pay for the wall, and approval from Congress, thereby acting contrary to the "faithful" execution the Office of President of the United States, by threatening the security of Americans, Mexicans living and working in the United, States, Mexican-American children born in the United States to undocumented parents, and the relationship between Mexico and the United States

**6.   A Narcissistic Personality Disorder is
"interpersonally exploitative – takes
advantage of others to achieve his own ends."**

Trump propagandizes "Fake News" as if
it were true, lies, misleads, starts rumors,
verbally attacks those who criticize or oppose
him, slanders and incites violence against Hillary
 Clinton, enables the "deplorables" within his
rabid ranks to make the most scandalous and
hate-filled anti-Hillary tweets, all for the sole
purpose of exploiting their fears and anger, to his
advantage.

**7.   A Narcissistic Personality Disorder
"lacks empathy, is unwilling to recognize or
identify with the feelings and needs of others."**

Trump announces he is going to let
"Obamacare implode," and with his personal
attacks on the existing healthcare system, Trump
forsook his oath to "faithfully execute the Office
of President of the United States, " in favor of a
dictator imposing his personal vindictive whims
 on the public -- their needs for healthcare
trumped by Trump's narcissistic ambitions. \

**8.   A Narcissistic Personality Disorder, "is
often envious of others or believes others are
envious of him."**

Trump, envious of Obama's presidency,
as Dubya was of Bill Clinton's becomes
obsessed with trashing, undoing, and defeating

all things Obama, with total disregard to its value to the United States. So for example, as Dubya dumped the Kyoto Accords, Trump ditches the Paris Agreement.

The issue is not the value, or lack thereof as to the Agreement, but rather that these two Narcissistic Personality Disordered Presidents would act personally outside the bounds of what the public expects of its President to self-indulge in their envy of their respective predecessor to devalue him, and the best interests of the public be damned!

9.   A Narcissistic Personality Disorder "shows arrogant, haughty behavior or attitudes."

One need only view Trump walking across the stage at one of his rallies, applauding himself, chin out, nose up, and lips pursed, to see an arrogant dictator, full of himself parading before his exploited, deliberately mis-informed, mad, and mislead masses,

Narcissistic Personality Disorder, like all personality disorders, is noteworthy for its pervasiveness -- its constancy -- always being exhibited – not a disorder or mental illness which can be turned on and off – comes and goes – No Dr. Jekyll and Mr. Hyde.

Literally all of Donald Trump's behavior – every action he takes and every word that he speaks and tweets is a manifestation of his narcissism, from his compulsion to hold rallies even AFTER he has been elected to his statement that his inauguration was the "largest ever," meaning all critiques, analyses, assessments, and discussions of Trump's policies, and politics made independent of his Narcissistic Personality Disorder, are as fatally flawed as a weather forecast without noting the temperature.

The evidence cited above, prove beyond reasonable doubt: (1) Donald Trump, having exceeded the criteria necessary for a diagnosis of Narcissistic Personality Disorder, is in fact a Narcissistic Personality Disorder. (2)Trump's disorder is both so debilitating and so pervasive as to render Trump incapable of loyalty or allegiance to any entity other than Donald Trump. (3) Trump's disorder precludes him from "faithfully executing the Office of President of the United States," meaning, (4) His oath of office was a hoax and a fraud, and (5) **Trump's continuing presidency as a *de facto* disloyal alien entity poses a serious threat to the internal and external security of the citizens of the United States, therefore (6) Trump must be declared mentally unfit, disqualified, and removed from office.**

<u>Count Three</u>

<u>Trump's Slanderous, and Seditious Attacks on President Obama Incites Trump's Followers to Establish an Alternative Government with Trump as Their Leader</u>

The following slanderous and seditious attacks made by Trump present clear and compelling evidence of Trump's incitement of his followers to depose President Obama and his government, and replace it with an alternative government with Trump as its leader.

"Made in America? Barack Obama called his birthplace Hawaii "here in Asia." 11/18/11

"Sadly, when it comes to using the energy industry to create American jobs, Obama has been a total disaster." 1/9/ 12

"Barack Obama hard at work yesterday shooting a marshmallow cannon in the WH East Room while our country burns." 2/8/12

"When I was 18, people called me Donald Trump. When he was 18, Barack Obama was Barry Soweto, Weird." 3/12 /12
They should have called you "Narcissus."

"I want to see Obama's college records to see how he listed his place of birth on the application." 5/30/12
We want to see your income tax records to see how many years you "stiffed" the IRS and the average American tax payer,

"Barack Obama is practically begging Romney to disavow the place of birth. He is afraid of it and for good reason. He keeps using John McCain as an example. However McCain lost the election. Don't' let it happen again." 5/29/12

"If Barack Obama had such a wonderful academic record why wouldn't he want to show it? 7/17/12.

"As I always said the "Birthers" were after the truth. Thanks to Sheriff Joe Obama can't hide anymore." 7/18/12.

""Congratulations to Real Sheriff Joe on his successful Cold Case Posse investigation which claims Barack Obama' Birth Certificate is a fake." 7/18/12

In the years 2012-2013, Trump tweeted **50 times** slandering President Obama that he was born in Kenya, forged his birth certificate showing he was born in Hawaii, lied about his Kenyan citizenship, lied that he was an American citizen, is therefore illegally President of the United States, and was involved in the death of the State Health Director who verified copies of Obama' birth certificate,

When all of Trump's outrageous, unconscionable, and seditions lies were debunked, was Trump man-enough to apologize in public to President Obama? Was Trump found liable for slander and libel, ordered to pay millions in damages,, and imprisoned for his seditious attack on the President of the United States?

No, on all counts. There may be "honor among thieves," but there is only dishonor from a Mafia-like thug whose money rules like a machine guns does for a "Godfather,"

"What is more important for the American public to have? Mitt Romney's tax returns or Barack Obama's sealed records? " 7/18/12
Neither – You're tax records.

"I am impressed with the scam Barack Obama pulled but the truth will come out." 7/20/12

"Weird – why did Barack Obama Sr. fail to list Barack Obama as his son in his 1961 INS application? 7/18/12

"In light the Benghazi emails released last night, it is apparent that Obama has no problem lying to the American public ..." 8/24/12

"An extremely credible source has called my office and told me that Barack's Birth Certificate is a fraud." 8/6/12

"An extremely credible source has called my office & told me that Barack Obama applied to Occidental as a foreign student – think about it." 8/6/12

"I wonder if Barack Obama ever had an Indonesian passport. Did he become an Indonesian citizen when he lived there? 8/9/12

"Why do Republicans keep apologizing on the so-called "birther" issue?

No more apologies – take the offensive,:
8/27/12

"Wake up America! See article "Israel: Science: Obama Birth Certificate is a fake"9/13/12.

"Obama is our unlucky President. Everything he touches turns into a mess. Some people just don't have it!" 9/17/ 12

"Obama's "07 speech which @Daily Caller just released not only shows that Obama is a racist but also how the press always covers for him." 10/3/12

"Once again Obama fails to classify China steal even more jobs and money from us. 10/15/12

"Barack Obama is not who you think he is. Most overrated politician in US history." 10/15/12

"Isn't it time that Obama release his college records and applications? Boy would that create a mess! He is not who you think." 10/15/12

"Because Obama was so pathetic in the first debate, tonight's audience will be humongous – people want to see if he is for real." 10/16/12

"I am happy to donate 45 million to a charity Barack Obama chooses. All I am asking is that he is transparent with the American people." 10/24/12.

"Obama has no problem leaking national security secrets. Why can't he release his records? Especially when $45M is going to charity?" 10/24/12

"Why does Obama believe he shouldn't comply with record releases that his predecessors did of their own volition. Hiding something? 10/30/12

Why is Obama playing basketball today? That's why our country is in trouble." 11/6/12

"Obama our Welfare & Food Stamp President, is praising himself for expanding welfare; He doesn't believe in work." 11/24/12

"Obama told the UN that the world is more stable than it was 5 years ago." Is he delusional?" 2/24/ 13

Obama has now become the weakest POTU against China, yuan just hit record high against dollar Very sad." 3/25/13

"Obama is not a leader, he's just a campaigner." 9/6/13.

" President Obama seems to be fawning and desperate to make a deal with Iran that lots of bad results can occur. Be cool and be careful. 9/19/13

"ObamaCare is a disaster and Snowden is a spy who should be executed – but if it could reveal Obama's records, I might become a major fan," 10/30/ 13

"I do not understand how so many of my Jewish friends backed Obama in the last election. He is a TOTAL DISASTER FOR ISRAEL – AND ALWAYS WILL BE." 11/24/13

"Obama is a disaster at foreign policy. Never had the experience or knowledge. He is not capable of doing the Job." 12/12/13

"How amazing, the State health Director who verified copies of Obama's birth certificate died in a plane crash today. All others lived." 12/12/13.

" Obama is about to embark on a vacation in his "native" Hawaii, putting Secret Service away from families on Christmas , Aloha!" 12/19/13

"President Obama, you are a complete and total disaster, but you have a chance to do something great and important, STOP THE FLIGHTS! 2/23/14

"President Obama was able to fool the Americans by getting elected, but not able to fool Vladimir Putin. Too bad for us." 3/20/14

"I don't hate Obama at all, I just think he is an absolutely terrible president. Maybe the worst in our history," 3/20/14

"President Obama looks absolutely exhausted in the Netherlands. He is not a natural leader, was never meant to lead. It is tough work for him." 3/25/14

"By Obama mentioning Manhattan yesterday in his response, he has singlehandedly made it target #1. How totally stupid is this guy?' 3/26/14.

"The way President Obama runs down the stairs of Air Force 1, hopping & bobbing all the way, is so inelegant and unpresidential. Do not fall." 4'22 14

""President Obama is losing on so many fronts, in fact all fronts, that I'm concerned he will do something totally irrational. He can't lead. 4/25. 14

"Obama is without a question, the WORST EVER president. I predict he will do something really bad and totally stupid to show manhood." 6/5/14.

"With our border not being secure, Obama is giving a pathway to terrorists to

enter our country. An attack is on him."
6/17/14

"Always remember I was the one who got Obama to release his birth certificate, or whatever that was. Hillary couldn't. McCain couldn't. 6/29/14.

"Obama looks exhausted and beaten. He was never made or prepared for the job. Like it or not, he doesn't have it." 7/9/14

"I believe that President Obama is so overwhelmed by what is happening in the U.S. and throughout the World that he has totally given up." 7/21/14

"If Obama resigns from office NOW. thereby doing a great service to the country--- I will give him free lifetime golf at any one of my courses." 9/10/14.

"Why are we sending thousands of ill-trained soldiers into Ebola-infested areas of Africa! Bring the plague back to U.S. Obama is so stupid." 9/19/14

"Despite the ever increasing Ebola disaster, Obama refuses to stop flights from West Africa. It's almost like he's saying F-you to U.S. Public." 10/7/2014

"President Obama has made one mistake after another for a very long time,

and the people of the United States are just
plain tired of it." 10/20/14

	"The new Ebola czar will report to the
WH &VASA adviser Susan Rice. More
mismanagement & duplicity with CDC.
Obama is a terrible executive." 10/17/14

	"Can you believe that President
Obama still hasn't stopped the flights and
people pouring into the U.S. from West
Africa. TERRIBLE PRESIDENT. 10/4/ 14

	"President Obama – close down the
flights from Ebola-infected areas right now.
before it is too late! What the hell is wrong
with you?" 10/4/14

	"Obama is looking like an incompetent
fool in the handling of the war against ISIS!
Why isn't China and Russia helping – they
gain so much!" 10/8/14

	"Obama won't send troops to fight
jihadists, yet sends them to Liberia to contract
Ebola. He's a delusional failure." 10/9/14

	"I was never a fan of Bush, in fact he
was so bad he gave us Obama. But Obama is
truly a pathetic excuse of a president, can't
get any worse." 10/20/14.

	'The United States under President
Obama has truly become the "gang that

couldn't shoot straight." Everything he touches turns to garbage," 10/21/14

"I have been saying for weeks for President Obama to stop flights from West Africa. So simple, but he refused, A TOTAL incompetent." 10/23/14

"President Obama has absolutely no control (or respect) over the African-American community – they have fared so poorly under his presidency." 11/25/14

"Sadly, because president Obama has done such a poor job as president, you won't see another black president for generations." 11/25/14

"ObamaCare to illegal's, yet wants to cut military benefits Disgrace," 12/4/14

"Obama now wants to deny due process to the police. He'll give constitutional rights to the terrorists but not our cops." 12/19/14

"The talks between the U.S and Iran are going on forever, WORLD"S LONGEST NEGOTIATION. Obama has no idea what he is doing –incompetent 2/23/15

"Pres. Obama was touting Yemen as a great success story – it just fell. Obama doesn't know what he is doing. Saudi Arabia is in big trouble." 3/26/15

" President Obama just had a news conference , but he doesn't have a clue. Our country is a divided crime scene, and it will only get worse," 7/17/15

"Christians need support in our country (and around the world), their religious liberty is at stake! Obama has been horrible, I will be great." 9/19/15

"President Obama said, "ISIL continues to shrink{ in an interview just hours before the horrible attack in Paris. He's just so bad." CHANGE. 11/14/15

"I. along with almost everyone else, have so little confidence in President Obama. He has a horrible attitude – a man who is resigned to defeat." 11/17/15.

'Is President Obama going to finally mention the word radical Islamic terrorism? If he doesn't he should immediately resign in disgrace." 1/12/16

"Interesting how President Obama so haltingly said, I "would never be president." – This from perhaps the worst president in U.S. history." 2/17/16

"In politics, and in life, ignorance is not a virtue." This is a primary reason that President Obama is the worst president in U.S. history!" 5/16/16

"President Obama thinks the nation is not as divided as people think. He is living in a world of the make believe." 7/10/16

"We are TRYING to fight ISIS, and now our own people are killing our police. Our country is divided and out of control. The world is watching." 7/17/16.

Not exactly. ISIS is the Sunni army which Dubya disbanded and threw out into the street to fend for themselves -- castrated, jobless, and disenfranchised under a new tyranny, aka a Sh'ia dictatorship.

Second, people retaliating against police murdering unarmed Africa-American males, are not people hunting and killing police.

Yes, our country is divided, and with every Trump tweet widens the division between Trump's "deplorables" – anti-Obama racists, white supremacists, neo-Nazis, para-military anti-government goon squads, and sundry hate groups, KKK'ers, and lost paranoids.

"Wow,. President Obama's brother Malik just announced that he is voting for me. Was probably treated badly by president-like everybody else." 7/24/16

"Not one American flag on the massive stage at the Democratic National Convention until people started complaining – than a small one – Pathetic." 7/27/16

"President Obama & Putin fail to reach deal on Syria – so what else is new? Obama is not a natural deal maker. Only makes bad deals." 9/5/16

"If Obama worked as hard on straightening out our country as he has trying to protect and elect Hillary, we would all be much better off." 11/4/16,

"Terrible! Just found out that Obama had my "wires tapped" in Trump Tower just before the victory. Nothing found. This is McCarthyism." 3/4/17.

"Ungrateful TRAITOR Chelsea Manning, who should never have been released from prison, is now calling President Obama a weak leader. Terrible." 1/26/17

"President Obama will go down as perhaps the worst president in the history of the United States." 8/2/16

No, Donald, 100 days into your presidency, and you not only seized the title of "Worst President Ever" from Dubya's living room mantle, but you also set the record for doing it in the shortest time. (It took :Dubya two years. and Nixon – now in third place on the 'Worst President Ever" list , took six years. Congratulations.)

(I predict Obama will be in the top ten of "Best Ever Presidents.)

That Trump would tweet, "President Obama will go down as perhaps the worst president in the history of the United State," with total disregard for the facts, provides another instance of Trump's arrogance, his self-indulgent sense of importance, and his peevish envy of President Obama.

But most alarming is Trump's shameless facility to lie – make up his own reality, AND expect his lies to be accepted as the unquestioned truth, at least among his faithful flock.

The truth, after 20 years of \\FOX NEWS – Conservative propaganda – "spin doctors," Reagan's bumper-sticker policy statements, lying Rehnquist, truth-bender Scalia, millionaire TV preachers Graham, Falwell, Roberts, Osteen, Robertson – masters of the art of lying -- every one-- telemarketers, Rush "Loose-Lips" Limbaugh, Karl "the Character Assassin" Rove, Dubya lying the United States into two fraudulent wars still being fought, two years of Trump's vituperative lying to get elected President, knowing Hitleresque lying was his key to the White House and now President Trump's vitriolic lying to cover up his previous lies, rampant bribery by NRA and corporate America, which, according to Chief Supreme Court Justice Roberts is not a crime, but only "the the way people now do business," lying, "fake news," and bribery, which by 2017, having been the *modus operandi* for Conservative Republican President Bush and Conservative Republican President Trump to achieve the highest status our Country allows simply by adhering to Hitler's counsel of the Big Lie:

"The size of the lie is a definite factor in causing it to be believed, for the vast masses of a nation, in the depths. of their hearts are more easily deceived than they are consciously and intestinally bad. The primitive simplicity of their minds renders them a more easy prey to a big lie than a small one for they themselves often tell little lies but would be ashamed to tell big ones. '—Hitler, *Mein Kamph*, 1935 --

We have become a land of liars, aided and abetted by the mythical "dignity of the individual," which decrees that the truth is what the individual says it is.

So if Dubya propagates the Big Lie: "Saddam Hussein has weapons of mass destruction" and I'm from Texas, or the South, or a Southern Baptist, or a Conservative Republican – Dubya's truth becomes my truth.

If Trump propagates the Big Lie that Obama was born in Kenya," and I'm a racist, or a white-supremacist,, or a neo-Nazi, or a KKK'er, or from Alabama, the South, or a Southern Baptist, or a Conservative Republican, I believe Obama, not Dubya is the reason I lost my job in the coal mines, Obama, not Dubya caused me to be foreclosed, Trump's truth becomes my truth, and anyone who calls Trump a liar is my mortal enemy who must be destroyed.

By the time of the election, Trump's propaganda had made America not great again, but like Germany in 1938 – again.

As H.L. Mencken observed, "The men the American people admire most extravagantly are the most daring liars -- the men Americans detest most violently are those who try to tell them the truth."

True to Hitler's instructions, Trump tweeted ""Bad Birther Obama," **50 times** between 2012-2013, so that by the time Obama ran for re-election in 2012, millions of white male voters in Red States, or the South, like my white racist, paranoid, high school drop-out neighbor, believed, "Obama was born in Kenya, Obama forged his birth certificate to get into Harvard where he rarely attended classes, would have flunked out if he had been white, Obama wouldn't have even been accepted at Harvard in the first place if he were white., and would never have been elected President if the public had known the truth that he was born in a foreign country.".

How was Trump able to have such an effect, however evil, on the American voter?

Trump learned, or more likely was instructed by Karl Rove wannabe, Brad Parscale, to tell the most outrageous lies – the more slanderous, despicable, deplorable, insulting and scandalous his lies – whatever it takes to get national news coverage 24/7 – name- recognition , however obtained, trumps all other strategies to get elected, at least in America, in 2016 -- A piece of cake for Trump whose narcissistic personality demands constant attention, constant ego-massages by an admiring public, and constant recognition of his unique superiority.

But, there is a dark side – a foreboding – Trump's violent, rampaging, armed, militant anti-government thugs on the streets of Charlottesville, Virginia, heirs to Hitler's renegade "brown shirts' loose on the streets of Berlin in the 1930's

Trump's outrageous, unconscionable, slanderous, and seditious attacks on sitting President of the United States Barack Obama, incites Trump's troops to overthrow President Obama and his government, thereby being a traitorous act, for which Trump must be charged, convicted, sentenced and removed as president.

<u>Count Four</u>

<u>Trump's Tweets Indict Trump as Being Loyal Only to Himself, and Therefore an Alien Threat to the   Government of the United States.</u>

Trump Tweets: "Sorry losers and haters, but **my IQ** is one of the highest – and you all know it.. Please don't feel so stupid or insecure; it's not your fault.' 5/8/13

"**I will** be the greatest job-producing president in American history." 1/23/16

"**I am the BEST** builder, just look at what I've built." 5/13/15

"**I am** attracting the biggest crowds, by far, and the best poll numbers, also by far. Much of the media is totally dishonest. So sad." 9/20/15

"Mitt Romney had his chance to beat a failed president but he choked like a dog. Now he calls me racist – but **I am** least racist person there is." 6/11/16.

"Many people have **said I'm the world's greatest** writer of 140 character sentences." 7/21/14

"Many are saying **I'm the best** 140 character writer in the world." It's easy when it's fun." 1l/10/ 12

:""**Nobody but Donald Trump will** save Israel. You are wasting your time with these politicians and political clowns, Best! 4/27/15

"**Nobody beats me** on National Security," 4/8/16

"Our Southern border is insecure. **I am the only one** that (sic) can fix it, nobody else has the guts to even talk about it." 7/3/15

"**I am** proud to have brought the subject of illegal immigration back into the discussion. Such a big problem for our country – I will solve." 8/26/15

"The only one to fix the infrastructure of our country is me – roads, airports, bridges. **I know** how to build, polls only know how to talk," 5/12/15.

"I am the only one that (sic) knows how to build cities – polls are all talk and no action. Our cities need help, and fast. They are crumbling!" 5/3/15

"Look where the world is today, a total mess, ISIS is still running around wild. **I can fix it fast**. Hillary has no chance." 5/20/16

"Just announced that as many as 5,000 ISIS fighters have infiltrated Europe. Also, many in U.S. I TOLD YOU SO! **I alone** can fix this problem." 3.24.16

"Love seeing union & non-union members alike are defecting to Trump. **I will** create jobs like no one else. The dem leaders can't compete!" 1/8/16

"It was great being in Michigan. Remember, **I am the only presidential** candidate who will bring jobs back to the U.S. and protect cur industry." 3/7/16

"If I run, I will be in all the primary debates and you will see why **I am** the only one who can Make America Great Again". 5/7/15.

"We will immediately repeal and replace ObamaCare – and **nobody can do that like me.**

We will save $'s and have much better
healthcare." 2/9/16

"Wow, the economy is really bad.
GROSS DOMESTIC PRODUCT down 0.7% in
first quarter – and getting worse.   **I TOLD
YOU SO!** Only **I can fix**." 5/29/15

"I am going to save Social Security
without any cuts. **I know** where to get the money
from. Nobody else does." 5/21/15

**'I know our complex tax laws better
than anyone** who has ever run for president and
I am the only one who can fix them." 10/2/16

"Another radical Islamic attack, this time
in Pakistan, targeting Christian women &
children. At least 67 dead, 400 injured**. I alone
can solve**." 3/27/16

"Hillary Clinton has been working on
solving the terrorism problem for years. TIME
FOR A CHANGE**, I WILL SOLVE** – AND
FAST!' 3/24/16.

" Govt. collapsing in Iraq only 2 weeks
after withdrawal of our troops, Sadly**, I called**
this one and please remember, **I alone called** it."
12.27/11

"One of the reasons **I am** no fan of John
McCain is that our Vets are being treated so
badly by him and the politicians, **I will fix VA
quickly." 7/18/15**

"**No one has done more for people with disabilities than me. I have** spent many millions of dollars to help out – and am happy to have done so." 2/9/16

"The media is so after **me** on women. Wow, this is tough business. **Nobody has more respect for women than Donald Trump.**" 3/25/16

"Wow, just saw an ad – Cruz is lying on so many levels. **There is nobody more against ObamaCare than me, will repeal & replace.** He lies." 1/31/16
\

Trump tweets: "**Nobody will protect our nation like Donald J. Trump.** Our military will be greatly strengthened and our borders will be strong. illegals out." 3/26/16.

"**Isn't it crazy that people of little or no talent or success can be so critical of those whose accomplishments (Trump's) are great with no retribution.**" 7/18/13

Isn't it crazy, **I'm worth billions** of dollars, employ thousands of people & get libeled by moron bloggers who can't afford a suit. WILD!" 2/19/ 14

"**I knew last year that Time Magazine lost all credibility when they didn't include me in their top 100.**" 10/26/12

'Face the **Nation's review of me was the highest rated show that they have had in 15 years.** Congratulations and WOW!" 1/11/16

Trump tweets: **"Trump SNL Episode Generates Highest Ratings Since 2012,: At the very least Donald Trump is making Saturday Night Live great again..** 11/8/15

"Chris Wallace interviewed me on Sunday, had his highest ratings since Feb of '09. Congratulations!: 10/22/15

"Chuck Todd just informed us that **my interview last week on Meet the Pr4ess was their highest rated show in 4 years..** Congrats!" 10/10/15

"Wow, the (my)ratings for 60 Minutes last night were the biggest in years – very nice." 9/28/15.

"Just announced that in the history of CNN last night's debate was the highest rated ever. Will they **send me** flowers & a thank you note?" 9/17/15

"Fox News you should be ashamed of yourself. I got you the highest debate ratings in your history & you say nothing but bad." 8/7/15

"Today in history WrestleMania 23," **I shave Vince McMahon's hair – highest rated show in WWE history."** 4/1/14

"Last week's Dateline, which **I hosted was the highest rated Dateline since January,"** 3/17/ 13

Trump tweeted: **"The Comedy Central Roast of Donald Trump last week was the #1 rated Comedy Central Roast ever …It brought in 3.5 million viewers."** 3/18/11

"Even though every poll, Time, Drudge etc, has **me wining the debate** by a lot. Fox News only puts negative people on. Biased – a total joke!" 2/4/16

Trump tweets""**The Trump base** is far bigger & stronger than ever before (despite some phony Fake News polling). Look at rallies in Penn, Iowa, Ohio." 8/7/15

Trump tweets: "Rubin Blogger, one of the dumber bloggers @ Washington Post only writes **purposely inaccurate pieces on me.** She is in love with Marco Rubio?' 12/4/15

"One of the dumber and least respected of the political pundits is Chris Cillizza one of the Washington Pot @ TheFix. Moron **hates my poll numbers."** 5/11/15

"The **Washington Post quickly put together a hit job book on me** –comprised of copies of some of their inaccurate stories. Don't buy, boring!" 8/22/15

""Wall Street Journal is bad at math. The good news is nobody cares what they say in their editorials anymore, **especially me."** 3/17/17

"When and how are the dummies at the Wall Street Journal going **to apologize to me** for their totally incorrect Editorial on me. I want "smart' trade deals." 11/12/15

"The ever dwindling Wall Street Journal which is worth about 1/10 of what it was purchased for, **is always hitting me politically. Who cares?"** 7/20/15

"I knew last year that Time Magazine lost all credibility when they didn't include **me** in their Top 100…" 10/26/12

"I guess Rupert Murdoch and the NY Post don't like Donald Trump. Such false reporting about my big hit in Iowa. Even my enemies said "bull." 1/28/15

"Wow**, I have always** liked the NY Post, but they have really lied when they covered **me** in Iowa. Packed house, standing O, best speech! Sad." 1/28/15

"Boring & failing NY Magazine's 3rd rate political reporter had flunky Dan Amira write **a totally false report about me** today … " 3/15/13

"NY Daily News, the dying tabloid owned by dopey clown **Mort Zuckerman, puts**

**me on the cover daily because I sell. My
honor, but it is dead.”** 6/28/15

“The failing NY Daily News which just
raised its prices because it’s dying, **said I wear a
“wig” when they know I don’t.** Dishonest.”
6/23/14

“The dying **NY Daily News asked me to
do an Editorial on the Central Park 5 ripoff *
then they pretend it was my idea.** Loser
newspaper!” 6/23/14

“**Wow, *I hear* Morning Joe has gone
really hostile since I said I won’t do or watch
the show anymore. They misrepresent my
positions!.”** 5/9/15

“ Just heard that crazy and very dumb
@morningmika had a mental breakdown while
talking **about me** on the low ratings@Morning
Joe. Joe a mess.”” 9/2/16

“**Is it possible for @megynkelly to
cover anyone but Donald Trump on her
terrible show, She totally misrepresents my
words and positions! BAD**.” 4/1/16.

Trump tweeted: “Everybody should
boycott the @megynkelly show. Never worth
watching. **Always a hit on Trump!** She is sick
& most overrated person on TV.” 3/18/16

“As dishonest as Rolling Stone is. **I say**
Huffington Post is worse. Neither has much

money – sue them and put them out of business!"
4/6/15

"The failing Huffington Post and dopey @ariannahuff are writing so much false junk about me—they just can't get enough! BE CAREFUL!." 8/12/13

" How can a dummy dope like Harry Hurt, who **wrote a failed book about me but doesn't know me or anything about me, be on TV discussing Trump?"** 7/29/15

"Dying @GQMagazine **just named me to list. Too bad**. GQ is no longer relevant – won't be around long."   12/2/13.

"The only reason Glenn Beck doesn't like me is I refused to do his failing show -- asked many times. Very few listeners – sad!" 1/22/16

"Frank Luntz is a low class slob who came **to my office looking for consulting world and I had zero interest.** Now he picks anti-Trump panels!" 8/7/15

Trump Tweeted: "Fox News is so biased it is disgusting. **They do not want Trump to win. All negative!"** 2/17/16.

"Pathetic attempt by Fox News to try and build up ratings for the GOP debate. **Without me they'd have no ratings!:**   1/26/16

"Few people know that Fortune Magazine is still in business. **Tell your writer Alisa Soloman that I left The Apprentice to run for president.**" 10/31/15

"**Really bad article about me** in the dying (or dead) Esquire Magazine. Totally false – lots of hatred. When will this boring magazine close?" 3/2/13

"The ultra liberal and seriously failing Des Moines **Register is BEGGING my team for press credentials to my event in Iowa today** – but they lie!" 7/25/25

"David Gregory got thrown off TV by NBC, fired like a dog. **Now he is on NN being nasty to me.** Not nice." 3/29/16

"Watched @davidaxlrod on @oreilly factor and the dog hit **me** even after **I made a big contribution to his charity. I never went bankrupt.**" 2/10/15

"**I heard** that the underachieving John King of CNN on Inside Politics was one hour of lies. Happily, few people are watching – dead network!" 7/10/16

"New Day on **CNN treats me very badly.** Alisyn Camerota is a disaster. Not going to watch anymore." 1/21/16

"CNN is unwatchable. **Their news on me is fiction**. They are a disgrace to the broadcasting industry and an arm of the Clinton campaign." 9/9/16

Trump tweets: "The CNN panels are so one-sided, **almost all against Trump**. Fox News is so much better and the ratings are much higher. Don't watch CNN." 7/24/1

Trump tweets:"CNN is the worst. They go to their dumb one-sided panels when a **podium speaker is for Trump**! VAST MAJORITY want: Make America Great Again!" 7/18/16

"Fox News is much better, and far more truthful than CNN which is all negative. Guests are stacked for Crooked Hillary! **I don't watch**." 7/17/16

"CNN is all negative when it comes to me, **I don't watch it anymore**," 6/27/16

"I am watching Fox News and how unfairly they are treating me and my words, and CNN and the total distortion of my words and what I am saying." 6/13/16

" I am watching CNN very little lately because they are so biased against me. Shows are predictable garbage! CNN and MSM is one big lie." 6/5/16

"@MajorCBS Major Garrett of CBS News **covers me** very inaccurately. Total agenda. Bad reporter." 1/11/16

"Watching biased Charles Krauthammer, a Fox News flunky, who didn't know that **I won every debate,** in particular -- the last one. Check polls!" 1/28/16
\

"Buzfeeds' McKay Coppins is a failed and dishonest reporter who refuses to mention the sarcasm **in my voice** when referring to him or irrelevant buzzfeed," 2/15/14

"Associated Press knowingly and inaccurately wrote about (my) Liberty University speech. Shameful reporting, no credibility." 9/26/12

"The liberal clown @ariannahuff told her minions at the money losing Huffington Post to **cover me as entertainment. I am #1 in Huff Post Poll."** 7/18/15

" Huffington Post is just upset that **I said** its purchase by AOL has been a disaster and that Arianna Huffington is ugly both inside and out." 4/20/14

(I) "Just watched Cookie Roberts on ABC. Her predictions have been so wrong for so long that she has lost all credibility. Just another sad case," 1/29/15

Trump tweets: "I hope all workers demand that their @Teamsters reps endorse **Donald J. Trump. Nobody knows jobs like I do.!** Don't let them sell you out." 1/8/16

"Nobody beats me on National Security." 4/8/16

"The economy is bad and getting worse – almost ZERO growth this quarter. **Nobody can beat me on the economy (and jobs).** MAKE AMERICA GREAT AGAIN," 4.30.16.

"The media is so after me on women. Wow, this is a tough business. Nobody has more respect for women than Donald Trump!" 3/26/16

"No-one has done more for people with disabilities than me. I have spent many millions of dollars to help out-and- am happy to have done so." 2/9/16

"Train wreck JUST THE BEGINNING. Our roads, airports, tunnels, bridges, electric grid – all falling apart. **I can fix for 20% of pols & better."** 5/13/15

"Look where the world is today, a total mess, and ISIS is still running around wild. **I can fix it fast. Hillary has no chance,"** 5/20/16.

"Just announced that as many as 5000 ISIS fighters have infiltrated Europe. Also, many in U.S. **I TOLD YOU SO.! I alone can fix this problem!"** 3/24/25

"Another radical Islamic attack, this time in Pakistan, targeting Christian women &

children/ At least 67 dead, 400 injured. **I alone
can solve."** 3/27/16.

" **I will be the best by far in fighting
terror. I'm the only one that was right from
the beginning & now lying' Ted & others are
copying me."** 3/23/16

**"I will be the greatest job-producing
president in American history."** 1/23/16

**"We need a President who isn't a
laughing stock to the entire World. We need a
truly great leader, a genius at strategy and
winning. Respect!"** (Me!) 8/9/14

**"I have long stated that Brian Williams
was not a very smart guy – all you have to do
is look at his past. Now he has proven me
correct."** 2/10/15

":**I've known** Chris Mathews for a long
time & sadly, he gets dumber each and every
year & started from very low base." 4/16/13

**"I hear that sleepy eyes Chuck Todd
will be fired like a dog from ratings starved
Meet the Press? I can't imagine what is taking
so long!'**   7/12/ 15

"Goofy political pundit George Will
spoke at Mar-a-Lago years ago. **I didn't attend**
because he's boring & often wrong – a total
dope!" 6/19/15

" Wacky Glen Beck who always seems to be crying (worse than Boehner) **speaks badly of me only because I refuse to do his show – a real nut job."** 10/8/15

"John Oliver had his people all to ask me to be on his very boring and low-rated show. I said, "NO THANKS" Waste of time & energy." 10/31/15

"'Everybody should boycott Megyn Kelly show. Never worth watching. **Always a hit on Trump**, she is sick and most overrated person on TV. " 3/18/16.

"I bet the dumbest political commentator on television Lawrence O'Donnell will soon be thrown off the air for poor ratings. He's a total looser – a face made for radio. (Already off Friday.)"2/3/12

:   Dope Frank Bruni said **I called** many people, including Karl Rove losers-- true**, I never** called my friend Howard Stern a loser – he's a winner!" 1/19/16

"I loved firing goofball atheist Penn@pennjillette on The Apprentice. He never had a chance. Wrote letter to me begging for forgiveness." 7/16/15

Trump tweets: "Marble mouth Tom Brokaw asks, "Why do we think to have a successful evening you have to have **Donald**

Trump as your guest of honor?" BORING
TOM." 8/27/13
\

"How does failed writer and pundit like
Stephen Hayes, with no success and little talent,
get away with criticizing candidates" **(Me)**
4/20/15

"Mitt Romney, who was one of the
dumbest and worst candidates in the history of
Republican politics, **is now pushing me on tax
returns, Dope!"** 2/25/16

(I'm) "Going to Ohio, home of one of the
worst presidential candidates in history – Kasich.
Can't debate, loved ObamaCare – dummy! "
11/23/15

"Can you believe the worst Mayor in the
U.S. & probably the worst Mayor in the history
of NYC, Bill de Blasio, **just called me a
"Blowhard!"** 11/20/15.

**"Lying Cruz put out a statement,
"Trump** & Rubio are with /Obama on gay
marriage." Cruz is the worst liar, crazy or very
dishonest. Perhaps all 3?" 2/11/16

"What a waste of time **(me)** being
interviewed by Anderson Cooper when he puts
on really stupid talking heads like Tim O'Brien -
- dumb guy with no clue!" 7/23/15

"**I am** going to keep our jobs in the U.S.
and totally rebuild our crumbling infrastru8cture.
Crooked Hillary has no clue!:" 5/7/16.

"Why is it Hillary Clinton's family and
Dems dealings with Russia are not looked at **but
my dealings are**?" 6/15/17

"Publicity seeking Lindsey Graham
falsely stated that **I said** there is moral
equivalency between KKK, neo-Nazis & white
supremacists'" 8/27/17

"After consultation **with my Generals**
and military experts, please be advised that the
United States Government will not accept or
allow Transgender individuals to serve in any
capacity in the U.S. Military. Our military must
be focused on decisive and overwhelming
victory and cannot be burdened with the
tremendous medical costs and disruption that
transgender in the military would entail. Thank
you." 7/26/17

"**I have** no second thought about ending
DACA,," (The Deferred Action for Childhood
Arrivals program.) 9/6/17

As can be readily gleaned from Trump's
tweets cited above, Trump's Narcissistic
Personality Disorder, defines a person whose
loyalty and allegiance is ONLY to himself and
who must ALWAYS act in his own self
interests, thereby preventing Trump from being
loyal and allegiant to the Government of the

United States and its Constitution, to which he swore to "preserve, protect and defend?

As such, Trump represents a clear and present danger to the internal and external security of the United States, -- just cause for Trump's removal from the Office of President.

<u>Count Five</u>

<u>Trump Commits Multiple Acts of Fraud And Violations of the Constitution.</u>

1.   January 20, 2017. **Trump':"Signs" His Fraudulent Contract with the Government of**

the United States and Its Citizens

Donald J. Trump swore or affirmed, *"I do solemnly swear that I will faithfully execute the Office of President of the United States, and will, to the best of my ability, preserve, protect and defend the Constitution of the United States."*

Fraud! Trump knew or should have known, that he had no experience, no training, and is unqualified to be President of the United States and was therefore precluded from "faithfully,' or otherwise, executing the Office of the United States."

Contracts obtained by fraud must be voided as a matter of law.\

Therefore, Trump's contract with the United States is null and void, he is not the President of the United States, his actions taken since January 20, 2017, must be voided, and the person who placed second in the Electoral College vote, must be awarded the presidency.

Fraud in the Inducement! Trump knew or should have known, that the promises, assurances, and representations he made to the American people in his "Contract" with the American voter, were the **province of Congress, not the President,** and therefore not promises he could or would keep.

Contracts obtained by fraud must be voided as a matter of law.\

Trump is 71 years old, and therefore old enough to know – even ignorant of his Narcissistic Personality Disorder -- that his loyalty and allegiance is to himself, and that he "had no others before" him -- certainly NOT the Government of the United States.

It follows that Trump is a *de facto* "foreign entity" – incapable of placing the interest of the United States above his self-interests. Beholden only to Narcissistic Personality Donald J. Trump, he has neither cause, nor interest in, preserving, protecting, and defending the Constitution of the United States.

Therefore, Trump's contract with the United States is null and void, he is not the President of the United States, his actions taken since January 20, 2017, must be voided, and the person who placed second in the Electoral College vote be awarded the presidency.

.

2.	January 23, 2017. **Trump Abuses
	Presidency by Dumping Trans-Pacific
	Partnership Deal to Insult Obama**

Trump campaigned; "The Trans-Pacific Partnership is another (Obama)_ disaster done and pushed by special interests who want to rape our country, just a continuing rape of our country."

The Patterson Institute, argued TPP would increase exports by $123 billion. The Obama administration estimated an increase of 650,000 jobs.

In truth, Trump's narcissistic envy of Obama decided the fate of TPP, and in so doing, Trump violated his contract with Americans to "execute' the Offices of the President of the United States" for the good and benefit of all Americans, NOT to satisfy his personal envy/jealousy of President Obama.

For having misused and abused his authority as President to personally demean an opponent, while compromising the interest of the United States, Trump invites the charge of breach of contract, to wit, failing to 'execute the Office of the President of the United States.

3.	January 27. **Trump Unconstitutionally Bans Refugees from Seven Islamic Countries for 90 days and Syrian Refugees. Indefinitely.**

Trump's ban violates the First Amendment prohibition against the "free exercise of religion ," in turn, violating Trump's contract to "preserve, protect, and defend the Constitution."

By banning one religion Congress "establishes" those regions not banned, also in violation of the Constitution of the United States.

Trump's ignorance, his lack of empathy, his haughty arrogance, which puts him above the law and therefore above the Constitution, or just Narcissistic Personality Disorder Trump being Narcissistic Personality Disorder Trump – entitled to do what he wants to whomever wants, when he wants, makes Trump an enemy of the State.

Oh, he's going to circumvent the Constitution – itself an offence – by pretending it's not a Muslim ban, but rather a ban on countries supporting terrorists?

Then why Iran, but not Saudi Arabia – homeland to 15 of the 19 9/11highjackers? Why Syria where immigrants are fleeing for their lives and most in need of safe harbor? Why Iraq, but not Afghanistan, which we invaded for allegedly training and sponsoring bin Laden's terrorists/?

By what calculus does Trump extrapolate that Muslims equal terrorists? Isn't it more likely that Trump's Muslim ban is a ruse to appeal to his evangelical base by "religious cleansing" – purging Muslims?

Another example of Trump exploiting the presidency to impose his will, whims, and wants on all Americans – satiate his delusions of greatness – more proof as to why Donald J. Trump, must be removed as President of the United States.

4.	February 7, **Trump Abuses the Power of the Presidency by Nominating Unqualified and Sworn Enemy of Public Education Betsy DeVos To Head Dept. of Education.**

In another narcissistic "middle finger" to Democrats, Trump willfully and maliciously nominates divisive Betsy DeVos to the top Education post in the government.

DeVos's claim to the throne is: (a) She's a major donor to Republican coffers, (b) She's an elitist – "Let them (the public schools) eat cake." (c) She's a sworn enemy of public schools, and (d) She'll really piss of the Democrats which titillates Trump with the same sadistic delight he gets saying the words, "You're fired,"

For the first time, a vice-president (Priest Pence) casts the deciding vote to break the 50-50 deadlock for a Cabinet nominee. (It is rumored, Trump was so delighted in once again sticking it to the Democrats, he wet his bed. "Fake News?)

5.	February 17._**Trump Violates His Oath of Office by Willfully and Maliciously Nominating an EPA Head To Eviscerate That Agency of the Federal Government.**

Once again Trump picks the most divisive candidate – the one most likely to rub salt into the wounds of the Democrats – another candidate nominated by Trump to satiate his narcissistic whim to stick it to the Democrats, the best interests of the Country be damned!

As Oklahoma's Attorney General, Pruitt had filed an estimated 20 suits against the EPA, the agency he is now going to lead, in but. another instance of Trump's malicious and treacherous abuse of power, acting so contrary to the interests of all Americans, as to rise to the level for which he must be removed.

6.	February 22. **Trump Abuses the Office of President to Personally Damage an Opponent By Reversing Obama's Bathroom Protections for Transgenders.**

In but another instance of Trump's narcissistic envy of Obama, this time rescinding Obama's Transgender bathroom protections – no reason given – just to misuse and abuse the role of President of the United States to vindicate his narcissistic envy of Obama, the effect on the lives of Transgenders being of no concern to Trump other than exploiting the bias of his base for political gain.

7..	February 24, **Trump Violates First Amendment Rights to a Free Press and Free Speech by Imposing a Press Ban**

By blocking certain media from a press conference, treacherously labeling the media "enemies of the American people," in turn, turning his "deplorables" into enemies of the State, Trump breaches his contract to "preserve, protect, and defend the Constitution of the United States.

During his campaign, Trump manipulated the media by his daily outrageous unconscionable, headliner, attention-getting ranting tirades and tweets, to trick the media into giving Trump FREE national coverage other candidates couldn't even afford to buy..

But now Trump is speaking as the President of the United States, rendering his same outrageous unconscionable, and headliner harangues to steal instant media coverage, to a higher standard. No longer can Trump's lies, propaganda, slander, libel, personal and petty attacks, threats, and demagogic diatribes be dismissed as just Donald being Donald. As the President, he is expected to speak for all Americans, not just to feed the gluttony of his base..

Furthermore, as a leader of a world power, Trump has leadership responsibilities as to our membership in the United Nations, as signer of treaties, and alliances, not as a Hitleresque rabble rouser.

We were wrong off course. Trump's Narcissistic Personality Disorder precludes him from ever getting outside his own skin – see his presidency other than a business he just took over '""hostile takeover" – fraudulent takeover, which he now owns and runs to his advantage. (Trump's non-union employees, by acquiescing to Trump's "loyalty pledge" are hired and fired at Trump's pleasure – his greatest pleasure being telling them, :You're fired!" And he thumbs his nose at charges of nepotism by making members if his immediate family *de facto* Board members and making deals as his way of doing business

Donald J. Trump, President of the United States is a *de facto* enemy of the United States, a threat to the internal and external security of the United States – a traitor, and must be removed as matter of law.

8., March 4. Trump's False and Fraudulent Statement That Obama Wiretapped Trump's Offices is a Crime Under 18 U.S.C. Section 1001.

Trump committed a crime under Federal Law, when he fraudulently stated as fact that Obama of wiretapped Trump's New York offices, when Trump knew there was no evidence to support the charges.

The court later ruled the case be dismissed for lack of evidence.

Trump must be charged with a Federal crime under 18 U.S.C. #1001, and removed from office.

Title 18.#1001(a)(2) reads in pertinent part: "…whoever, in any matter within the jurisdiction of the executive branch of government of the United States knowingly and willfully …makes any materially false, fictitious or fraudulent statement …shall be fined…imprisoned not more than 5 years …"

9. March 6. Trump Signs Second Unconstitutional Immigration Ban.

Having had his first ban declared unconstitutional, Trump signs Ban #2 reducing the number of Muslim countries prohibited from

sending their immigrants to the United States
from seven to six, but still failing to justify
which countries are banned and which are not.

Trump's arbitrary standard is purported to
be the risk to the United States of a terrorist
attack posed by these countries, yet, Afghanistan,
is not included despite being invaded by Dubya
for having trained and given safe harbor to bin
Laden terrorists. Saudi Arabia is not included
despite having trained and exported 15 of the 19
suicide bombers of the World Trade Center on
9/11, revealing that Trump's ban is an abuse and
misuse of the Office of the President of the
United States for personal gain -- a deal struck in
which Trump exploits anti-Muslim hatred for
political gain, while playing "footsy" with the
oil-rich Sunni Saudis.

10.   March 11. **Trump's ex- National
Security Advisor Michael Flynn Attended
Intelligence Briefings with Candidate Trump
while Lobbying for Turkey.**

Flynn and Trump participated in "secret"
intelligence meetings while Flynn was being paid
half a million dollars as a Turkish lobbyist. Then,
as Trump's National Security Advisor Flynn
played a role in the US Government's policy
toward Turkey.

By Executive Order of January 28, 2017,
Trump banned Executive Branch appointees
from lobbying for five years.

It would seem Trump makes up the rules
and enforces them as he chooses.

11.   April 7. **Trump violates International, Federal, and United Nations Law by Launching Missiles at Syrian Base.**

On Trump's orders at 7:40 p.m., on Thursday, April 7, 2017, 59 Tomahawk Missiles are launched against Syria from United States destroyers in the Mediterranean,

Does the United States even have the right to attack a country which has not provoked, or threatened us? Does Trump care, or is this but just another example of Donald being Donald – entitled to do whatever strokes his narcissism at the moment?

Article 1, Section 8, Clause 11 of the U.S. Constitution grants Congress the power to declare war. The President meanwhile derives the power to direct the military AFTER a Congressional declaration of war from Article II Section 2, which names the President Commander-in-Chief of the armed forces.

Exceptions to the rule are allowed during armed insurrections and rebellions as in the attack on Fort Sumter, South Carolina by armed Confederates, or an attack on the United States by a foreign entity, to wit, Japan's attack on December 7, 1941.

Article 51 of the U.N. Charter provides for the "inherent right of self-defense if an armed attack occurs."

The War Powers Act of 1973 refers to the use of armed forces being dispatched abroad by the President, who must notify Congress within 48 hours.

As no troops were dispatched by General Trump, provisions of the War Powers Act are irrelevant.

A reasonable and prudent person, would therefore conclude: (a) Trump acted precipitously on "reports" without verification from other disinterested sources, (b) Trump acted irresponsibly by not first conferring with our allies. (c) Trump acted dangerously by not considering the response from other countries and entities already at war in Syria, (d) Trump appears to have been insouciant to the possibility of Syrian terrorist reprisal attacks on Americans abroad and at home. (e) Trump violated international law and Article 51 of the UN Charter by attacking a country which had not first attacked, or threatened to attack the United States .(f) Trump's bombing was an act of war, which Trump did NOT have the authority to do. (g) Trump's knew, or should have known, the internal affairs of a sovereign nation are not the province of the United States.. (h) Trump's concerns about war crimes allegedly committed by President Bashar al-Assad should have been referred to the UN and the War Crimes Tribunal at the Hague. (i) Trump's illegal bombing of Syria, like Bush II's illegal bombing of Iraq has the look, smell, and feel of a narcissistic bully waging war to satisfy his gluttony for glory..

The letter from Trump to Congress justifying his bombing of Syria was improper, demeaning of Congress, untimely, and an admission of violating the Constitution, international law, and the United Nations

Charter, for which Trump should have been prosecuted and removed.

12.   April 10. **Trump Violates Constitutional "Guarantee" of a "Fair and Impartial Judiciary" In Gorsuch Supreme Court Appointment**

In his rush to pat himself on the back for having fulfilled a campaign promise – as if the mere act of fulfilling was a good thing regardless of the merits, or lack thereof, of the substance of the promise -- an always hyperbolic Trump announces at a Rose Garden photo-op, "And I got it done in the first 100 days –You think that's easy?/" (And exactly what did you do Donald other than submit Gorsuch's name to a Republican-controlled Senate, which had already made the nomination of Gorsuch possible by violating their sworn oath to "preserve, protect, and defend the Constitution of the United States" by refusing to consider an Obama's Supreme Court nominee?)

But Trump, basking in his own self-imposed halo, continues his grossly exaggerated achievement: "This ceremony has a special meaning as Justice Gorsuch is filling the seat of one of the greatest' (Narcissistics only think in superlatives – "greatest," as in "I'm the greatest President," and "worst: as in, "Obama is the worst President in the history of the United States," leaving the listener no choice but to dismiss both statements and all that follow), "Supreme Court judges in American history, and that's Antonin Scalia. Who is a terrific – was a

terrific judge and a terrific person … a patriot
who revered our Constitution .. beloved by
many…he is deeply missed by all of us,"

(The listener must assume sports
announcer wannabe Trump is ignorant of the fact
that Conservative extremist Scalia was a leader
of the "Gang of Five," who criminally interdicted
Florida's election rules, voided their recount, set
aside the winner of the popular vote – Al Gore,
for the sole illicit purpose of putting one of their
own Conservative Republicans in the White
House – Dubya "The- Debauched Bush."
(Clarence Thomas, appointed by Dubya's daddy
also failed to do the right thing – recuse himself.)

And it was smiling Constitution assassin
Antonin Scalia who gave comfort to the NRA
and gun –crazies, by willfully misapprehending
the Second Amendment phrase "well-regulated
militia" to mean, every nut-case, psychopath,
Neo-Nazi, White-Supremacist, Trump
"deplorable," KKK member, rejected lover,
cheated wife, Right-To-Lifer, bar room brawler,
alcoholic, drug abuser, and angry neighbor has a
constitutional right to bear a loaded weapon.

Bingo! Americans own more guns and
kill each other with guns more than any other
country not at war. (The funeral directors of
America are eternally grateful to Antonin.)

And it was Conservative Republican
Fundamentalist extremist Scalia, who by his
dominating bullying, in the "Citizens United"
case, issued the preposterous self-serving, purely,
political ruling that corporations are people, and
as such, pursuant to Scalia's profane and
perverted interpretation of the First

Amendment's right to free speech, can make
unlimited donations – bribes – to politicians,
political parties, organizations and PACs --
guaranteeing Republicans a future playing field
titled in their favor in all future elections.

As a result of Scalia's political meddling,
wealthy Republican donors control governments
as never before, one-man-one-vote is quashed,
lobbyist's bribes make and pass laws, members
of the 10% club control the 90%, who now
become more and more disenfranchised, and
America slips away from being a Republic to an
oligarchy – government of the rich, by the rich
and for the rich.

Trump continues, "He (Gorsuch) will
decide cases based not on personal preference,
(just as Trump does routinely), but a fair and
object reading of the law." (Donald, we will
grant you only that it is unlikely Brother Gorsuch
will decide cases as subjectively as you would, in
that you would be 100% biased for your self-
interests, and incapable of looking at any issue
outside the parameters of your narcissism. That's
what Narcissistic Personalities like you do.

Otherwise, Trump's self-serving dinosaur
feces aside, if Gorsuch was going to decide cases
according to a "fair and objective reading of the
law," as Trump herein advertises, (a) Trump
would not have   nominated him in the first
place, and (b) the Conservative Republican-
controlled Senate would not have confirmed him.

Trump lied. Trump knew he lied,
Another fraud upon the American citizenry.

From saying so during his campaign that
Trump would nominate a Supreme Court Judge

based on how close the nominee came to fitting in Scalia's shoes, Trump nominated Gorsuch because he presumed Gorsuch was just such a Scalia Conservative extremist Fundamentalist. The only difference between Gorsuch and Scalia being that Gorsuch is without the loyalty and allegiance to the Roman Catholic Church.

By knowingly nominating a Scalia-like judge and by confirming his nomination, Trump and the Republican Senators (plus three Democrats), conspired to violate the Constitution's guarantees of a "fair and impartial judiciary".

13..   April 16._**Trump's Demand of an Investigation into Tax Day Demonstrators is Fraudulent, an Egregious Abuse of Presidential Authority, and Misuse of Presidential Power for Personal Gain.**

Trump tweets that the protesters in 150 cities across the country were "paid protesters. The election is over. Someone should look into who paid for the small organized rallies."

Narcissistic Personality Disorder Trump, deluded that he rules as if he were Pope or Charles V, believes he owns the Government of the United States – that it is his to do with as he chooses, this time to punish those protesting his refusal to disclose his income taxes, as every other president has done.

This misuse and abuse of presidential power is the stuff of kings, some of who were beheaded, or shot, for similar abuses.

We, a more civilized lot, ask only that Trump be removed from office, his head attached.

14,   April 26. **Trump's Order to Review – (revoke) Federal Monuments and National Parks, Specifically Obama's Bears Ears National Monument in Utah, is Another Misuse of Presidential Power to Settle Personal Scores.**

In but another attempt to dismantle all of Obama's achievements, while putting money in the pockets of the already rich, and under the ruse of "States' Rights," Trump orders a "review:" -- in truth, a surreptitious plan to pilfer public lands to profit private ranching, logging, mining, and drilling interests.

Trump announces, "Today we're putting the states back in charge. The states should decide which land is protected and which is open for development."

Oh. like the states can invade a women's body to decide the outcome of her pregnancy?

Apparently, Donald is no student of history. From 1630-1776, each colony made up its own "local" rules. and from 1776 to 1865, the "states" were in charge -- the :"States' Rights" legacy being Apartheid southern-style – on a continuum of crimes against humanity with ethnic genocide and the Holocaust,

Since the end of the Civil War– wars never end, only soldiers end -- America's bloodiest war – 625,000 killed from a population of 32,443,000, southern states, refusing to accept defeat in their illegal secession, use the

foil of "States' Rights" to perpetuate Apartheid
underground

Trump, a racist, "State's Rights" agitator,
whose *blitzkrieg* of Executive Orders borders on
a seditious usurpation of Congress by a Nixon-
like imperial president, adds, "Obama's use of
the 1906 Antiquities Act to create monuments
was an "egregious abuse of federal power" that
allowed the federal government to "lock up
millions of acres of land and water."

But Trump fails to explain what Obama
or the Government gained from "locking up
millions of acres of land and water." He didn't
need to. President Teddy Roosevelt set the
precedent for Presidents to conserve and protect
federal land for the pleasure and recreation "good
"of all Americans.

And Trump's reason for unlocking
Federal Monuments and National Parks,
specifically Obama's Bears Ears National
Monument in Utah? MONEY.

With Trump it is always about TRUMP
and MONEY—Trump gets to stab Obama in the
back one more time, and he puts MONEY in the
pockets of his rich confederates in the ranching,
logging, mining, and drilling business.

Republican Utah governor and the State's
delegation opposed Obama's Bears Ears
monument, arguing it got in the way of private
development,

THAT's WHY THE STATES CAN"T
BE TRUSTED TO DESIDE ON WHICH LAND
TO SET ASIDE, dumb ass Donald!

15.   April 28. **Trump Willfully and Maliciously Misapprehends Second Amendment to "Guarantee" NRA Most Favored Status.**

Preaching to the choir – gun rights, penis-envy, NRA, crazies in Atlanta, Trump decrees, "The eight-year assault"(by Obama) "on your Second Amendment freedoms has come to a crashing end … You have a true friend and champion in the White House …. I will never infringe on the people to keep and bear arms. Never ever." **(The NRA bribed Trump with a buyout three times more than the NRA spent to bribe Romney.)**

The parents of the 20 six and seven year children massacred at Sandy Hook Elementary School in Newtown, Connecticut on December 14, 2012,by a 20-year-old schizo, using a Bushmaster Model XM15-E2S rifle, and carrying a semi-automatic.223 caliber rifle, and two handguns, must have viewed Trump's sell-out and salute to the NRA, as enabling more Sandy Hook massacres.. (If those parents didn't, I did.)

An Izhmash Saiga 12, 12 gauge semi-automatic shotgun was found in the mass murderer's car. All weapons were bought legally by the shooters mother, Nancy Lanza, begging the question who was the crazier and most criminally liable for the murder of those 20 children and six women teachers and staff: (1) The 20 year-old schizo shooter, (2) His mother who he killed before going to the school,(3) the gun store owner who sold the weapons to Nancy

Lanza, and who should have notified the police as to the quality and quantity of the weapons sold,(3) The NRA, whose bribing of Republican, Conservative, and southern politicians, results in a self-serving private company making public policy as if it were an agency of the Federal Government, (4) The politicians who took the NRA bribes, treacherously called "campaign donations," and//or, (5) The Supreme Court bully, false profit, and self-anointed Court Pope, Antonin Scalia, who by dominating the hearts and minds of the heartless and mindless Conservative judges, in a deliberate and malicious misapprehension of the Second Amendment, on June 26, 2008, opined "militia" meant "individual"?

(Did anyone review Scalia's bank statements?)

In the 5-4 majority opinion, written of course by Pope Scalia, he decided that the "operative clause" was "The right of the people to keep and bear arms shall not be infringed," thereby following the Conservative "dirty trick" of cherry-picking words and phrases from the Constitution (AND their Bible) to support their biases and preconceptions, while simply "forgetting' omitting, or deleting those words and phrases which exposes their myths, lies, deceptions and misconceptions.

The operative clause of the Second Amendment -- "operative" if for no other reason that it comes first, and which Scalia and his confederates pretend doesn't exist states, "A well regulated Militia, being necessary to the security of a free State…"

That first clause—those first 13 words, provide the REASON for bearing arms – as being "necessary to the security of a free State" – the common good -- to allow for a Militia – a group of men to defend against a foreign attacking force, so each adult male in the household can grab his musket over the mantle and join his similarly armed neighbors to repel an invading soldiery – The Brits.

Scalia and his "Gang of Four" Conservative confederates, knew that: (1) nowhere in the Second Amendment does it declare, imply, or intend that a "Well regulated" means an "individual," (2) Nowhere in the Second Amendment does it state, imply, or intend that a."Militia" means an individual, (3) Nowhere in the Second Amendment does it state, imply, or intend that a "free State" means one person, and nowhere in the Second Amendment does it allow,. imply, or intend that "arms" meant more than a single shot musket – not an arsenal of assault weapons capable of killing 20 six and seven year old school children in a matter of seconds.

Finally, shameless unconscionable Connecticut Superior Court Judge Barbara Bellis, forgetting that the doctrine of fundamental fairness and justice is the reason for the law, rather than the law being the tail wagging the dog of justice, dismisses the parent's lawsuit against the gun maker Remington, the gun dealer, Camfour -- the company that owned the gun store, and Riverview Sales, who sold the assault rifles to the mass killer's mother.

History tells us Judge Bellis, having ruled for business and against the Sandy Hook parents would have summarily dismissed a case against Scalia and his Gang of Four Supreme Court judges, whose willful and political misapprehending of the Second Amendment in June, 2008, was the direct and proximate cause of putting a Bushmaster Model XM15-E2S assault rifle in schizo Adam Lanza's hand.

Trump, with no time or interest in connecting the massacre of 20 children killed as a direct result of NRA's bribery of Republican and Conservative politicians, callously claimed, "You have a true friend and champion in the White House …. I will never infringe on the people to keep and bear arms. Never ever."

For having willfully and maliciously misapprehended the Second Amendment of the Constitution, Trump breached his contract to "preserve, protect, and defend the Constitution., for which Trump should be removed as President.

For having willfully and maliciously misapprehended the Second Amendment of the Constitution, Trump conspired with a private company – the NRA – to endanger the lives of Americans, for which Trump should be removed as President.

For having willfully and maliciously misapprehended the Second Amendment of the Constitution, Trump conspired with a private company – the NRA – to enable more Adam Lanza's to gain access to weapons of mass destruction for which Trump should be removed as President.

16.	April 30. **In CBS Interview, Trump Fraudulently Accuses China in Democratic Committee Leaks.**

Without any evidence, Trump claims China, not Russia, hacked the emails of the Democratic Committee to meddle in the 2016 election, thereby aiding and abetting, and embarrassing Hillary Clinton just before the election.

Trump knew his allegation implicating China was at odds with the consensus of US intelligence officials and that he was perpetrating fraud in a crude ruse to detract the focus of the hacking investigation from Russia to China.

Trump would later blame the leaks on Democrats, the Democratic Committee, President Obama, Edward Snowden, Steve Bannon, White House staff, the *Washington Post, The New York Times*, "Fake" News," and the media,

Trump's fraud enforced by his puppet Attorney General Sessions, is that whistle-blower leaks, enjoined by "classified information" leaks, fuse into patriotic insiders exposing Trump's lies, fraud, deceptive government practices, and incompetence with spies – Bob Woodward with Julius Rosenberg.– a treacherous attempt by Trump and Sessions to purge dissenters, for which Stalin became infamous.

For having made knowingly false and fraudulent accusations, Trump is liable for a felony conviction under U.S.C. 18 #Section 1001.

17..   May 8. Trump Fraudulently Tweets "Russia Collusion Story is a Total Hoax, When Will This Taxpayer Funded Charade End?"

Trump's tweeted presidency is a fraud, con, and hoax, in which Trump's tweets: (a) Circumvent answering reporter's questions, (b) Totally control the communication, (c) Violate the American citizen's right to know, and (d) Subvert the democratic principle of an enlightened electorate into the propaganda forum of a dictator.

Methinks Trump doth protesteth too much. If he believed it was indeed a hoax, he would go about the business of "faithfully executing the Office of President of the United States," confidently knowing truth would prevail

As for pretending his concern is for the taxpayer, all but the most "deplorable" of his base, must by now realize this simple unequivocal truth: Donald J. Trump's sole interest is Donald J. Trump.

18.   May 9. Trump's Firing of FBI Director Comey – Obstruction of Justice 18 U.S.C.   Chapter 73 #1513(e)

While FBI Director James Comey was addressing a FBI business meeting in Los Angeles, he received notice via national TV that Trump had fired him. and later, by a hand-delivered letter in an envelope, in which Trump wrote, "While I greatly appreciate you informing me, on three separate occasions that while I am not under investigation, I nevertheless, concur with the judgment of the Department of Justice that you are not able to effectively lead the Bureau.'

This from the same Trump who had been repeatedly seen on TV crossing the room to embrace Comey, and otherwise give the appearance of impropriety by whispering words to the effect, "Can I count on your loyalty,: which in Trumpese, means, "Back off your investigation of me as to Russia and Putin, or else!"

In a clumsy attempt to do an end-run around the conventional wisdom that Trump fired Comey because Comey was being "disloyal," to wit, Comey refused to "back off " from investigating "Putingate," Trump assigns responsibility for firing Comey, to his Attorney General, Jeff Sessions, who himself has already been found guilty of lying to Congress about his own Russian contacts as a member of Trump's Transition Team.

Session in turn implicates Assistant Attorney General Rod Rosenstein's three-page memo critical of Comey's FBI leadership.

But Trump's treacherous hiding behind hit man Sessions and junior hit man Rosenstein backfires, when the media now moves its spotlight away from haloed Donald's hallowed ground to Sessions and Rosenstein.

Trump will overlook, incompetence, admitted backgrounds in the KKK, neo-Nazi and white supremacy groups, and will even pardon criminals, (the convicted Sheriff in Arizona), but DO NOT EVER upstage Donald – steal his thunder – replace him as the center of the world's attention!

No self-respecting Narcissistic Personality would tolerate such impertinence -- such a violation of the Narcissi tic's Code of Conduct.-- "Off with their heads!"

Not exactly. Trump simply has both Sessions and Rosenstein jerked off the stage by announcing he (TRUMP) and he alone fired Comey.

Not only had Trump done the firing ,but he had made up his mind to do so weeks before he heard from either Sessions or Rosenstein./

Knee-jerk narcissistic jerk Donald does indeed regain the national media attention, but at a price – Trump's non-base is more convinced than ever that Trump fired Comey because Comey had ignored Trump's threat to back off from investigating the suspected conspiracy between Trump and Putin to rig the 2016 presidential election so that Trump wins and Hillary loses.

Title 18 U.S.C. Chapter 73 Section 1513(e) reads."Whoever knowingly, with the intent to retaliate, takes any action harmful to any person, including interference with the lawful employment or livelihood of any person, for providing to a law enforcement officer any truthful information relating to the commission or possible commission of any Federal offense, shall be fined under this title or imprisoned not more than 10 years, or both."

What goes around, comes around. Trump, who ran for the Office of President of the United States hawking the BIG LIE "Convict Hillary," will soon be legitimately hawked as "Convict Trump"

19.	May 11. **Trump Signs Fraudulent Order to Create Commission to Investigate Trump's Unfounded Claim of Voter Fraud.** \\

With no evidence and with no support other than from "Yes Man," Bobble-Head, sick sycophant, Protestant Pope Pence and Kansas' paranoid Secretary of State Kris Kobach, deluded Donald, convinced that the presidential election of 2016 was "rigged; signs an Order legitimizing his delusion and at taxpayer' expense.

Fearing he would lose the election, Trump warned that the election was rigged against him and for Hillary, when he knew, or should have known, rigging was done by the Russians for him and against Hillary,

After he won the Electoral College vote, Trump tweeted, "In addition to winning the Electoral College in a landside, I won the popular vote if you deduct the millions of people who voted illegally. for Hillary."

To the naive person on the street, Trump's claim that he would have won the popular vote but for the millions who voted illegally for Hillary is just another example of crazy Donald being crazy Donald.

To his base, faceless Pence, and Steve "Bad Man" Bannon, Trump's charge of ubiquitous voter fraud will be proven correct.

To the pundits, his claims will be discussed as more erratic inexplicable Trump behavior.

To the careful reader, Trump's charge that three million illegal votes were cast for Hillary, is beyond absurd – scary – alarming that the President of the United States is so deranged and dangerous! We have no choice but to remove Trump. The Republic and its citizens demands it!

To any psychologist or psychiatrist, Trump's paranoid delusion that three million voters voted "illegally" for Hillary Clinton is precisely how a Narcissistic Personality Disorder would deny the reality of having lost the popular vote.

For having abused his presidency by issuing this fraudulent Order, Trump invites the charge of disqualification from the Office of the presidency due to mental defect.

20..   May 12.**Trump's Tweets That Written Statements Replace WH Briefings, Thereby Violating Citizens First Amendment Right to a Free Press and The Citizen's Right to Know.**

Trump creates storms of contradiction, reversals, and misstatements which his crew – staff, can neither fathom nor make intelligible to the press attending briefings.

Trump being narcissistic Trump, blames his staff for his bad press, explaining, "A very active President with lots of things happening it is not possible for my surrogates to stand at

podium with perfect accuracy."
you have a level of hostility that's incredible.
And it's very unfair."

"Unfair' in Trump's dictionary means
less than devout praise of Trump.

The problem he alleges his staff has with
being "perfectly accurate" in their description of
Trump's actions, statements and tweets is due to
Trump's inaccuracy in stating the facts, for
example, first claiming he fired FBI Director
Comey based on the recommendation of
Attorney General Sessions, next on the report of
Assistant Attorney General Rod Rosenstein, and
next Trump claims he had made up his mind to
fire Comey weeks before Session's
recommendation or Rosenstein letter calling for
Comey's firing,

"In fact when I decided to just do it, I said
to myself, I said you know this Russia thing with
Trump and Russia is a made-up story; it's an
excuse by the Democrats for having lost an
election that they should have won."

Trump's evidence for such an outrageous
irresponsible statement? None.

**Trump's problems with the press are
due solely to Trump's problem with the truth.**

The solution is not to do away with the
daily press briefings, or firing his Press
Secretary, but rather accompanying each of
Trump's statements and tweets with the results
of Trump's lie-detector test.

For Trump's to intend that written
statements replace WH briefings, in addition to
violating First Amendment rights to a free
press and citizens' right to know, reveals an

alarming summarily dismissal of the Bill of
Right, the Constitution of the United States, and
the relationship between that government and its
people, making it obvious that Trump will never
be an appropriate President to the Republic and
MUST be removed.

21.   May 12. **Trump Threatens Comey To
Hope No Tapes of Their Conversations Exist.**

Trump tweets, "James Comey better hope
that there are no "tapes" of our conversation
before he starts leaking to the press," thereby
impugning Comey's honesty, threatening Comey
to cease and desist commenting on their
conversations. and fraudulently implying that
Comey's statements relating to those meetings
rise to the level of criminal leaking of classified
information.
Others opine that Trump's threats to
intimidate, bully, and muzzle Comey to be a new
instance of Trump's criminal obstruction of
justice – a felony requiring removal from office
as a matter of law and the founding principle that
"no man is above the law.".
18 U.S. Code 1512(b) provides,
"Whoever knowingly uses intimidation,
threatens, or corruptly persuades another person,
with the intent to influence. or prevent
the testimony of any person in an official
proceeding, or withhold testimony from an
official proceeding, shall be fined under this title
or imprisoned not more than 20 years or both."
Trump must forthwith be indicted.

22..   May 16. **Trump's "Sharing Counter-Terrorism Information with Russia's Lavrov Compromises America's Security and Trust of America's Sources**

Referring to a meeting with Russian Foreign Minister Lavrov and Russian Ambassador to the United States Kislyak, Trump tweets: "As President I wanted to share with Russia (at an openly scheduled WH meeting) which I have the absolute right to do, facts pertaining to terrorism and airline flight safety Humanitarian reasons, plus I want Russia to greatly step up their fight against ISIS & terrorism."

Trump's National Security Advisor H.R. McMaster, predictably claimed that the story that Trump offered the two Russians classified information is "false.," contradicting Trumps tweets that he had the "absolute right" to share facts pertaining to terrorism and airline flight safety…"

The *Guardian* reported that Trump shared Israeli intelligence with the two Russians about an ISIS plot to use bombs placed inside laptop computers to bring down plains, thereby compromising US national security, Israeli intelligence, and putting Syrian sources at risk.

The *Guardian* quotes. John McCain: "Regrettably, the time President Trump spent sharing sensitive information with the Russians was time he did not spend focusing on Russia's aggressive behavior, including its interference in American and European elections, Russia's illegal invasion of Ukraine and annexation of

Crimea, its other destabilizing activities across Europe, the slaughter of innocent civilians and targeting of hospitals in Syria."

In any event, Trump's "sharing" counter-terrorism information with Russia's leaders suggests Trump's security clearance be revoked, rendering him unsuited to be President, in turn grounds for removing him.

23.   May 16. **Trump Commits Felonious Perjury When He Denies He Asked Comey to End Investigation of Flynn.**

At a Senate Hearing, former FBI Director James Comey testifies that during a meeting with Trump on February 14, 2017, Trump asked Comey to "close down" the FBI's investigation of Michael Flynn, Trump's National Security Advisor,

Trump fired Flynn on February 13, for misleading Vice-President Pence as to Flynn's contacts with Russian Ambassador Kislyak

So who do we believe? Trump who lies with callous flippancy and whose presidency may hang in the balance of Comey's investigation, or Comey, who is an honorable man with nothing to gain by acknowledging Trump directed Comey to back off his investigation of Flynn?

Only fools, Trump's "deplorables," or Trump's phalanx of parasites would deter an investigation of Trump on the charge of felonious Obstruction of Justice under 18 U.S. Code 1512(b)!

24..	May 30. **Trump's Proposal to Abandon Senate's 60-40 vote to 51-49, to "Speed up Health Care Legislation" Violates Fundamental	Rules to Rig the Process in Trump' Favor.**

King Donald I, deluded he IS the Rule, now makes up his own rules – change the process so that he can ram his bills and laws through Congress.

Needing only a simple majority, and with both the House and Senate controlled by the Republicans, Trump's changing the process strikes at the heart of the fundamental role of the minority in establishing balance in the government.

Furthermore, Trump trespasses into the Congress' yard, violates the principle of "checks and balances;" abuses his role as President to bully Legislators, and violates his contract to preserve, protect, and defend the Constitution, any one offense being worthy of censure and removal

25.	June 12. **Attorney Generals from Maryland and DC Sue Trump Alleging Violations of Constitution's Emolument Clause.**

The Emolument clause prohibits President Trump from accepting gifts or benefits from foreign governments. The suit contends that Trump's decision to retain ownership of his empire, makes him liable by profiting from foreign governments staying at Trump's hotels and resorts, thereby making him susceptible to foreign influence.

26.   June 16. **Trump Abuses and Misuses his Presidential Authority and Violates his Contract to Faithfully Execute the Office of President by Making International Policy to Personally Demean and Insult President Obama by Rolling Back Obama's Removal of Restrictions of Travel to Cuba,**

What a pitiful sight!! Grown middle-age groveling men in suit and tie, led by bishop bobble head Pence, applauding, as if by command, Trump as he signs his Order placing restrictions on Americans traveling to Cuba – driveling, drooling, deadheads, deigning, dutifully to divest themselves of any dignity -- their noses a fecal brown as they witness their mentally disturbed President continue his envious assault on all things Obama – the wishes and interests of the American people and the needs of the Cuban people be damned!

27.   June 23. **Trump Cuts $400,000 Funding for "Life After Hate" -- a Non-Profit Group For People Leaving the KKK, White Supremacists and Neo- Nazis Groups, Thereby Violating Congress's Constitutional Role in All Matters of Funding, and Revealing Trump's Support for Groups Plotting the Overthrow of the Government Trump was Hired to Protect.**

And why would closet racist, White-Supremacist, neo-Nazi, Trump, pretending, like Attorney General Sessions, and Bad Boy Bannon, to be a Populist, want to discourage his brothers in the business of promoting hate and overthrow of the government from abandoning their loyalties and affiliations?

Trump wouldn't. Trump didn't, and by his actions of adhering to these groups, who by their actions and pronouncements declare themselves to be enemies of the United States, and by giving these hate groups "aid and comfort within the United States," <u>Trump is guilty of treason and shall suffer death, or shall be imprisoned not less than five years … and shall be unable of holding any office under the United States</u> ." (18 U.S. Code # 2381 - Treason.)

28.	June 28. **By holding a 2020 Presidential Campaign Rally at Trump International Hotel in DC, Trump Demonstrates His Contempt for the Rules of Engagement and His Love of Self.**

Trump raises a reported $10 million from his guests attending his $35,000. 00 per plate 2020 fundraiser at his hotel on Pennsylvania Avenue, a stone's through from the White House.

There is no indication that any of Trump's blue-color base were invited or attended.

As with everything Trump does, this fundraiser has the look, feel, and smell of impropriety. First, the public expects their

President to be busy learning about the business of governing, putting staff in place and meeting with our allies during the early days of his presidency, particularly when that President has no experience in government or governing.

Second, Trump knew or should known, it is vulgar, boorish, and unpresidential, to so soon, and so prematurely, beginning raising money for re-election, when he's only been President for 180 days.

Third, by holding a fundraiser requiring participants pay $35,000 per plate renders his "Populist" title a fraud and a con,

Fourth, a $35,000 per plate fundraiser was a bullying tactic to intimidate Democrats.

29.   July 1. Trump Threatens States Which Refuse to Submit Some or All of the Requested Voter Information Demanded by Trump's Trumped Up Presidential Advisory Commission on Voter Fraud.

Trump tweets, "Numerous states are refusing to give information to the very distinguished VOTER FRAUD PANEL. What are they trying to hide?"

CNN reports that 44 states and the District of Columbia have refused to comply with Trump's dragnet Order.

This is a most compelling example of the financial cost to the American taxpayer caused by Trump's Narcissistic Personality Disorder and the cost of the lost confidence Americans will have in their elections,

The facts are these. (1) Trump lost the popular vote by just under 3 million votes. (2) Narcissistic Personalities cannot simultaneously delude themselves of their invincibility AND acknowledge defeat. (3) Trump's only choice is to claim Hillary's three million more votes resulted from "MASS VOTER FRAUD." (4) The "very distinguished Voter Fraud Panel," is distinguished only because it was singularly created to indulge Trump in his delusion of omnipotence -- nothing more -- nothing less. (5) As such, it is a fraud perpetrated by Trump on the American public. (6) Trump has bullied and intimidated Americans into a lose-lose situation – if we indulge Trump in his Fraud, we'll have to bear the cost of his sham Voter Fraud Panel. If we refuse, Trump will continue his propaganda attack on our election process, in turn, undermining future elections.

.	And there is no Republican male other than John McCain, and no Republicans other than Susan Collins, and Lisa Murkowski with the courage and integrity to order Trump to play in his sand box, play by the rules, and begin acting in the best interests of all Americans, or do the right thing – that which is best for the United States of America RESIGN.

30.	July 24. <u>Trump Disgraces the Office of President of the United States By Exploiting Boy Scouts at THEIR Jamboree by Making It Into a Political Forum.</u>,

Narcissistic Personality Disorder, self-inflated, bad mannered, exploitative Donald J.

Trump disgraces the Office of the President of the United States by shamelessly turning, what should have been a speech inspiring the boys to love their country into a speech about why they must love Donald J. Trump.

The *Washington Post*'s Katie Mettler and Derk Hawkins noted "Trump's Boy Scouts Speech Broke with 80 years of Presidential Tradition," after recalling FDR's speech about "good citizenship," Truman's "extolled fellowship," Eisenhower's invocation regarding "bonds of common purpose and common ideals," and Bush I's focus on "serving others," Trump, standing before 40,000 (Boy Scouts) "bragged about the record crowd size, bashed President Barack Obama, criticized the "fake media" trashed Hillary Clinton's presidential campaign, and threatened to fire his health and human services secretary if he couldn't persuade members of Congress to vote for the Republican health-care bill"

In truth, Trump could not address the 40,000 Boy Scouts as the President of the United States because he is no more than the titular President – otherwise acting for, and on behalf of, Donald J. Trump. Because of his Narcissistic Personality Disorder his loyalty and allegiance is now, and will always be, to Donald J. Trump and never to the United States and its Constitution,

So it was on that afternoon on July 24, 2017, standing before 40,00 Boy Scouts in Glen Jean, West Virginia, with a giant American flag behind him, Donald J, Trump proclaimed, his inability to execute the Office of the Presidency of the United States.

Looking beyond Trump's effrontery to 80 years of presidential precedent, beyond Trump's exploitation of 40,000 Boy Scouts, and beyond Trump's boorish bad manners and his delusion of self-importance, the simple inexorable truth is this: **Donald J. Trump will NEVER "faithfully execute the Office of the President of the United States and preserve, protect, and defend the Constitution because his Narcissistic Personality Disorder renders him loyal only to himself – *a defacto* foreign entity as if he were born and raised Russian. As an alien entity, Trump represents a threat to the internal and external security of America, and must be removed from the presidency of the United States.**

31.   July 26. Trump's Order that "the United States Government Will Not Accept Transgender Individuals to Serve in Any Capacity in the US Military." Violates U.S. Code Title 42 Chapter 21

Trump tweets, "After consultation with my generals and military experts, please be advised that the United States Government will not accept or allow Transgender individuals to serve in any capacity in the U.S. Military. Out military must be focused on decisive and overwhelming victory and cannot be burdened with the tremendous medical costs and disruption that transgender in the military would entail. Thank you.' (Three separate tweets sent at 8:55 AM, 9:04 AM and 9:08 AM July 26, 2017.)

Trump's violation of federal law aside, Trump's edict says much about the character of President Trump – his sadistic pleasure in inflicting ruthless pain on those who oppose him --Republican candidates, Obama. Hillary Clinton, James Comey -- those who criticize him – CNN, FOX, Huffington Post, Washington Post, NY Times, *et al* -- Democrats, and those who worked for (with) him – Attorney General Sally Yates. Michael Flynn. Katie Walsh, Michael Duke, Walter Shaub, US Attorney Bharara and 19 other US Attorneys, Spicer, Angella Reid, Michael Short, Derek Harvey, Anthony Scaramucci, Reince Priebus, George Sifakis, Steve Bannon, and Tom Price – those Trump has threatened to fire – Attorney General Sessions and those he would fire if he could -- Mitch McConnell and Paulo Ryan --- minorities -- African-Americans, Mexicans, immigrants, Muslims, counter-protesters – his bullying, his contempt for laws and rules, his arrogant presumption that he is superior to everyone else and therefore entitled to make up his own rules, his abuse and misuse of the presidency to settle personal peeves, achieve personal gain, and to increase the size of "Trump's Troops," and, as to the present instance, his lack of empathy – callous lack concern for those Transgenders currently in the military,. with no plan how to implement the ban, and no thought given to the effect of his edict on the military and society.

According to *the New York Times,* Defense Secretary Mattis received only a one day notice of Trump's decision and that Trump's sudden decision was made to interdict a fight between two opposing sides – social Republican Conservatives dismissive of all people not straight, not using the missionary position once a month whether in heat or not, and LGBT/Transgenders.

Trump attempts to justify his prejudice against LGBT's with the specious claim that the government's agreeing to pay for Transgender's "sex operations" represents the government's support of these "deviants.", On the other side, are those who supported Obama's anti-discrimination Order of Transgenders in the military.

At stake Trump's increased defense budget.

Enter Trump's tweet. revoking Obama's Order banning transgender discrimination -- POOF! No more Transgender issue.

Not so fast. U.S. Code, Title 42, Chapter 21-Civil Rights – prohibits discrimination against persons based on gender, age, disability race, national origin m and religion.

Trump's Order that "the United States Government will not accept Transgender individuals to serve in any capacity in the US Military." **violates U.S. Code Title 42 Chapter 21!**

Trump has once again violated federal law, thereby adding to the body of evidence that he must be removed.

32.   August 11, **Trump's Threat to Intervene Militarily Against Venezuela is Unconstitutional   as was His Threats to Bomb North Korea.**

Narcissistic Personality Trump needing to appear as king of the hill on the world's stage just as Bush II had done, looks to pick a fight with Venezuela's President Nicolas Maduro citing, "Venezuela is not very far away and the people are suffering and they're dying. We have many options for Venezuela, including a possible military option if necessary."

Hold it right there King, Emperor, Generalissimo Trump! Your delusion of becoming Donald "The Great" ends where the United Nations Charter and Congressional approval begins. Even Narcissistic Personality Disorder Bush II, had the fortuitous 9/11 attack and had conned the UN into believing the BIG LIE that Saddam Hussein had chemical weapons and weapons of mass destruction as pre-conditions to invade Iraq.

You not only have none of these justifications for war or illicit invasion, but you have four more reasons to butt out of Venezuela's internal affairs; (1) No other nation will support or follow your lead. (2) Having lied so often to the American people, nothing you could tell them would be believable enough to compel them to die in Venezuela on your account. (3)Eight months of observing your total inability to govern your own country, and (4) Most compelling, Congress, NOT the President, has the power to declare war and to invade a foreign country.

Therefore, Trump's Threat to Intervene Militarily Against Venezuela (and North Korea) violates the Constitutional, doctrine of "separation of powers," and Article 1 Section8, Clause 11 of the Constitution which grants Congress the power to declare war, in turn, giving good cause to remove Trump.

33..   August 25. **Trump's Pardon of Convicted Arizona Sheriff Joe Arpaio, Although Legal, May Still be an Impeachable Offense and Grounds for Removal.**

With a self-loving smirk on his face, an arrogant, presidential Trump, "shoots the bird," at America's judicial system, craps on his own Department of Justice, mocks the Founding Father's fundamental principle of "no man is above the law," contradicts Trump's oft-repeated rants for State's Rights. and further enrages the poor and minorities by confirming that American has two systems of justice – a punitive, prison-centered one for the 90%, and a free pass for the rich and privileged 10%.

Speaking out of both sides of his mouth is the least of Trump's offenses. (This is the same Trump who campaigned on slandering Hillary Clinton as "Killer Hillary," and "Convict Hillary," knowing he had no evidence to support his slanderous and libelous attacks, yet he now pardons a real "Convicted Joe"!

Convict Sheriff Arapio gained national attention for his sadistic and brutal mistreatment of immigrants, racial profiling, false arrests, and hunting Mexican immigrants as if they were rabid coyotes.

Trump now justifies his intrusive, politically motivated, shameless pardon of

"Sheriff Joe, " as "pay-off for Joe's racist, white supremacist, bigoted, "hate crime," of falsely and slanderously charging that Obama's birth certificate was a forgery, falsely claiming Obama was born in. the Kenya, not Hawaii.

Trump, in 2012, wrote on top of a news clipping about Joe being investigated for his abuses of power, saying, "Joe -- Great going – You're the only one with the guts to do this –" (Investigate Obama's allegedly "forged" birth certificate).. "Keep up the good Fight" --

July 18, 2012. Trump tweets; "Congratulations to @RealSheriffJoe on his successful Cold Case Posse investigation which claims @BarackObama's birth certificate is fake," (Big Lie! Obama's certified birth certificate showed he was born in Hawaii, not Kenya as Trump, Sheriff Joe, and Trump's Troops had falsely claimed.)

And again two hours later, Trump tweets: "As I always said, the "Birthers" were after the truth. Thanks to @RealSheriffJoe @BarackObama can't hide anymore."

So there you have it in Trump's own words –Trump admitting he is a vile racist, white-supremacist, KKK, neo-Nazi, Hitleresque propagandist, hiding behind the seemingly benign title of "Populist."

Just as Paranoid Personality Hitler fraudulently induced the German people to elect him President in 1934, Narcissistic Personality Trump fraudulently induced the American people to elect him President in 2016.

Which country suffered the greater tragedy remains to be seen

Article II. Section 2 of the Constitution: The President shall have the power to grant reprieves and pardons for offenses against the United States, except in cases of impeachment."

Historically, the presidential power to pardon was an act of compassion or mercy:, to wit, (1) Correct judicial overreach -- Carter pardoned 200,000 Vietnam War draft evaders. (2) Remedy a miscarriage of justice – Obama shortening the sentences of prisoners of non-violent crimes, and (3) To serve the "public's interest" -- Gerald Ford's bogus rationale for pardoning Nixon, was so at odds with the public's view of the "public's interest" that Republicans lost 50 seats in the House of Representatives that year and Ford lost the election two years later.

Trump's pardon of convicted Arizona Sheriff Joe Arpaio, being to personally repay Sheriff Joe –" the "Birthers," fails the test of being "merciful," fails the test of righting an "injustice" and fails the test of being in the "public's interests."

To the contrary, Trump's pardon of "Convicted Joe," is an abuse of presidential authority, an egregious and treacherous misapprehension Article II. Section 2 of the Constitution, divisive in its profanity, so contrary to the public's well-being and trust of the presidency, as to rise to the level of a crime under 18 U.S.C. #1001 (a)(2) – knowingly and willfully making false statements, punishable by fines and 5 years in prison.

34..   August 28. **Trump Signing of an Order Reversing Obama's' Restrictions on Sending Military Weapons & Gear to Local Police & Sheriff Shows Such Depraved Indifference to the Common Good and Failure to Execute the Office of President as to be Just Cause for Removal**

As the result of the public's outcry of seeing armored military vehicles and police armed with assault weapons on the streets of Ferguson , Missouri, making it seem as if the police were at war with the those protesting the police shooting of an unarmed African-American Michael Brown, President Obama restricted the sale of military weapons to local police.

President Obama reasoned that by creating an "at war" atmosphere, the police increased the violence rather than quelling it. "We've seen how militarized gear can sometimes give people feeling like they (the police) are an occupying force,"

,If Obama was for a reduced police state, knee-jerk Trump would be for a police state. Besides, racist, closet white-supremacist, neo-Nazi sympathizer, law and order, kick-ass,, "Sheriff Joe," comrade, Donald Trump makes no distinction between the local cop on the neighborhood beat , border guards hunting humans as if they were wolves, and the soldier fighting ISIS in Iraq.

Most importantly, Trump has the narcissistic delusion of being all-powerful, and must sell this delusion to the fearful, naïve, anesthetized American each and every day.

Wonder-wimp and trigger-happy racist Attorney General Sessions, steals Trump's thunder by boasting that as a result of Herr Trump's Order, local police will have grenade launchers, high-caliber assault weapons, bayonets and even armed aircraft.

(Trump received five deferments during Vietnam War – four college deferments and one medical. He reportedly played football, tennis, squash and golf in college, yet somehow managed to get a medical deferment after his college deferments expired – "bone spurs in his foot," but years later couldn't remember which foot, why it had never bothered him while playing sports, was never treated, and the "disabling condition" never showed up in any subsequent exams.(Money changed hands between Trump's daddy and a crooked Army doctor).

Sessions also never served in the military, other than playing soldier one weekend a month as a reservist, making both Trump and Sessions "Sunshine patriots" at best, and otherwise treacherous imposters. which should cause Americans sleepless nights with trigger-happy Trump as their Commander in Chief.

35..   August 31. **By Ordering a 90% Cut in Affordable Care Act Funding, Trump Violates Article 1, Section 9 of the Constitution.**

Article 1, Section 9 – The Appropriations Clause; "No Money shall be drawn from the Treasury, but in Consequence of Appropriations made by Law, and a regular Statement and Account of the Receipts and Expenditures of all public Money shall be published from time to time," thereby giving the "power of the purse" to Congress as the final arbiter in the use of public funds.

FOUL!! Trump can't repeal and replace Obamacare legitimately, so he breaks the rules, violates the fundamental principle of checks and balances and "separation of powers", thereby threatening the very existence of the Republic, and moving another step closer to becoming a dictator. Off with his head!!

Well, no -- not in 2017 - Just Trump's removal from the Office of President for violating his contract to "preserve, protect, and defend the Constitution," for his abuse and misuse of the power of the presidency to influence legislation, and Trump's abuse and misuse of presidential authority to achieve personal vindictiveness against former President Obama..

,

36.   September 1_ **By Designating September 3rd as "Day of Prayer," this Least of Christians Among Us -- President Trump Violates The   First Amendment of the Constitution.**

Ordaining himself "Bishop Trump," whose next act of Christ-like, empathy and compassion for anyone other than himself will be his first, Trump proclaims September 3 as a "Day of Prayer," and by so doing, Trump misuses the Office of President to exploit the victims of

Hurricane Harvey for political gain, adds "hypocrite" to his rap sheet of sins and "high crimes and misdemeanors,' and violates the First Amendment provision against the establishment of religion.

Taken together they must be considered grounds for removal

37.   September 1. **The Department of Justice Finds No Evidence to Support Trump's Charge that Obama wiretapped Trump's Offices.**

Neither the Dept. of Justice, nor the FBI found any evidence to support Trump's claim that then President Obama had wiretapped Trump's phones in Trump Towers in New York, as Trump had alleged.

The penalty Trump will incur for his multiple acts of slander, libel and making perjured statements to Federal officials -- the felonious crime of Perjury under i8 U.S. Code Section 1621 – a maximum penalty of five years in federal prison.

When may Obama and the American public receive an apology from President Trump? When will Trump become "Convict Trump?"

The answer to the first is "NEVER!" Trump is a Narcissistic Personality Disorder deluded he is NEVER wrong, and too much the thug to apologize. The answer to the second question is: "Not soon enough."

38.   September 5 By Ordering The Dept. of Homeland Security to Immediately Stop Accepting Applications' for DACA, Trump Abuses and Misuses the Office of President to Personally and Maliciously Trash Another Obama Program with no Reason Other than to Defame Obama -- the Benefit to 800,000 "Dreamers" be Damned!

Once again, Trump demonstrates his Narcissistic Personality's sadistic pleasure in telling some 800,000 immigrant children arrivals to the US, that they may now be deported .

Knowing his sidekick Sesssions gets the same sadistic sense of power and enjoyment kicking around the "little people" --African-Americans, Native Americans, immigrants, and children, Trump grants Sessions the fun experience of announcing that those 800,000 immigrants who came to the United States as children and who were protected from deportation by Obama's2012 Executive Order, will no longer be protected.

Trump may be excused for his cruelty, his shameless lack of empathy, and seeing the plight of others as something to be exploited, but ex-Eagle Scout, Southern Methodist – the worst kind of Methodist -- Holier-than-Thou, Bible-pounding, Sunday school teacher, Sessions, needs to explain to the American people he is supposed to be serving, how he reconciles Christ's message, "Suffer little children to come unto me, and forbid then not, for such is the kingdom of heaven, " with his rush to deport these 800,000 who came "unto" the US as little children to end their suffering. … We're waiting Jeff …

Accusing Obama's Protection order as being an "open-ended circumvention of immigration laws," just further exposes Sessions for the being the false prophet – the anti—Christ, southern Bible-pounding, phony fraud he has always been.

Meanwhile, we have another instance of Trump abusing and maliciously misusing the presidency of the United States to personally besmirch the character and influence of former President Obama.

39.	September 19. **Trump Addresses UN. General Assembly -- No Crime Other Than Disgracing of the Office of President, Disgracing Trump Himself, and Putting All Americans at Risk by Provoking Our Enemies and Making Defectors of our Friends**

Trump addresses the UN General Assembly as if he was performing at one of his rallies. Problem: Instead of preaching to his choir of true-believers his lies, "fake news, spins" and propaganda, Trump faces stone-faced country leaders prepped for Trump's gross exaggerations, bombastic diatribes, and offensive personal attacks.

Trump did not disappoint. He insulted berated, and baited North Korea leader Kim Jong-Un, calling him ?Rocket Man," threatened to "totally destroy North Korea," labeled Iran as a "corrupt dictatorship," whose "chief exports are violence, bloodshed, and chaos,: and accused the Venezuela President of having inflicted terrible pain and suffering on the good people of that country."

Iran's foreign minister countered, Trump's speech was an "ignorant hate speech (which) belongs in medieval times," Venezuela's foreign minister duly noted, "Trump is not the president of the world." (True, but he thinks he is.)

Swedish Foreign Minister Margot Wallstrom opined, "It was the wrong speech at the wrong time, to the wrong audience."

Sarah Snyder, associate professor at American University's School of International Service observed, "Reading the text of the speech, I was struck by the extent to which the language he's (Trump's) using is potentially more appropriate for schoolyard debates as opposed to what we normally see on the floor of the UN General Assembly … Using language like "loser terrorists" as Trump described terrorist groups strikes me as not the most compelling way to make an argument about international policy."

CNN characterized Trump's speech: "Trump is at root, a provocative. He likes causing controversy. He likes stirring the pot, He likes freaking out the squares. And, he likes using his 30+million followers on Twitter as a sort of focus group for his lines. "Rocket Man" got a big response – so he wanted to use it again…he sends a signal that he is tough, unafraid and keeping all options on the table, and that makes it a victory for him whether or not the consequences from his words are anything close

to what he hopes they will be. That's Trumpism
– pure and unadulterated."

Hillary Clinton, appearing on "The Late
Show with Stephen Colbert" called Trump's
speech ,"very dark, dangerous" and "not the kind
of message that the leader of the greatest nation
in the world should be delivering."

Trump's daddy, Newt "The Newt'
Gingrich, progenitor of Narcissistic Personality
Disorders in American politics, describes
Trump's speech as an "intellectual call to arms
…reminiscent of Winston-Churchill's warnings
against European appeasement of Hitler…"
(Newt, still the same slippery, pompous,
narcissistic, pseudo-intellectual, character
assassin, deplorable Newt! Much has been
written and said about Trump – he'll say and do
anything to grab attention – but no one until
Newt would use the words "intellectual" and
"Trump" in the same sentence.)

Breitbart News -- FOX News --
Conservative Propaganda 24/7 on steroids, and
microphone for Bannon's strident palaver, claims
Trump's speech was "a return to form that
should give hope to his "America first' base."
(Fecal matter! "America First" means Trump
First!).

MSNBC's Lawrence O'Donnell offers,
"Nuclear war with North Korea has been
unthinkable – to every president except the
untrained, ignorant and frighteningly dangerous
man who is now the president of the United
States."

William Saletan, writing for *Slate.,* states.
"…the United Nations General Assembly …was

lectured by an authoritarian, a torture apologist, a pillage enthusiast, a race-baiter, and a sectarian demagogue …But this time, the despot, the demagogue, and the war-crimes advocate had something in common. This time they were all the president of the United States…just another populist thug … not to make a case for universal rights, but to glorify nationalism."

(Isn't the most flattering phrase to describe Hitler's Nazi's was "glorifying nationalism?")

In fact, all critiques, all analyses, and all attempts to "spin" defend, or condemn Trump are fatally flawed – like judging a person by the color of their skin – a woman by the dress she's wearing, or a dessert without tasting it – the proverbial book by its cover?

Freud maintained that one's personality is determined by age six, our personality being the essence of who we are – that entity emerging from all that we have observed, experienced, and felt during those first six years – the story about us as we tell it to ourselves in the words and feelings of a child, which explains why personality disorders are so resistant to therapy – By age 20, 30 ,40,50, they've been living that personality every hour of every day for all those years, during which they interpret current events as confirmation of their story finished by age six.

So it was on Tuesday September 19, 2017, Trump stood at the podium before the United Nations General Assembly, first and foremost as a Narcissistic Personality Disorder, NOT as President of the United States, NOT as representing his country's membership in the

United Nations, and NOT having any loyalty or allegiance to any entity other than to Donald J. Trump, all of which makes him more, not less, dangerous as a loose cannon – "breach loaded and ready to fire!"

Speaking to the United Nations General Assembly graced Trump's delusion of grandiosity and his fantasy of superiority. Of course he would simultaneously disrespect the other heads of state and their surrogates, while believing he is entitled, by his inherent deluded superiority, to expect respect from them.

Of course, Trump would insult, bully, and threaten Kim Jong Un, and castigate Iran's and Venezuela's leaders – It's what Narcissistic Personalities do – put others down to increase their sense of self-importance. (Recall Trump tweeting, "Obama is the worst President in American history, and "Killer Hillary.")

Of course, Trump will demonstrate a total absence of care or concern for the feelings, beliefs, or needs of any of the UN countries in attendance. (Criterion #7 for a diagnosis of Narcissistic Personality Disorder – "Lack of empathy –unwilling to recognize or identify with the feelings and needs of others".)

Of course, Trump is going to promote – neo-Nazi nationalism – "America First" – automatically grants Trump "World First", *uber alles* as it did Hitler.

Trump's delusion of grandiosity could receive no greater affirmation.. (Are you paying attention, Newt? I'm talking to you about Donald and to you about you.)

And although Hitler was more likely a Paranoid Personality, that difference in diagnosis does nothing to dissuade us that Hitler's "brown shirts," do not set a precedent for Trump's Troops -- 30 million neo-Nazis, para-military. white-supremacists, racists, neo-nationalists some of whom were marching with Trump-Pence signs in Charlottesville, Virginia on August 11-12.

(Speaking personally, I fear a Trump lead gang of armed thugs much more than leaderless disillusioned radicalized Muslims.)

Trump addresses the United Nations General Assembly -- no crime other than disgracing the Office of President, disgracing Trump himself, and putting all Americans at risk by provoking our enemies and making defectors of our friends, still suffices as a recommendation for the removal of Trump for having been a speech Hitler could have made in 1938.

Count Six

Trump's Support for Neo-Nazis, Neo-Nationalists, Neo-Confederates, White Supremacists, Racists, Anti-Semites,, Anti-Muslims, Anti--Immigrants, para-military hate groups, KKK'ers – Those Individuals Threatening the Overthrow of the Government of the United States Makes Trump a Traitor, who Must be so Charged and Removed from Office.

The Unite the Right rally in Charlottesville, Virginia, on August 11-12, 2017, was sponsored, supported and attended by white supremacists, KKK members, neo-confederates, neo-Nazis, neo-nationalists, anti-Semites, and anti-Muslims pumping anti-Muslim and anti-Semitic banners, sundry para-military groups -- many armed with semi-automatic rifles, wearing swastikas, carrying Confederate battle flags , and chanting white supremacists and neo-Nazi slogans, and **TRUMP SUPPORTERS**, waving Trump-Pence signs – this latter fact notably absent from most accounts and reports,

The Rally purportedly was to protest the removal of the Robert E. Lee monument from Emancipation Park, which had itself been recently renamed from Lee Park.

Violence breaks out between the far right protesters and counter-protesters, leaving one killed, and 39 injured.

Virginia Governor McAuliffe declares a state of emergency. Soon State police arrive to announce the assembly was now unlawful.

Around 1:45 on the afternoon of August 12, 2017, an adult male affiliated with one of the right-wing groups drives his car into a crowd of counter-protesters, killing Heather Heyer, a 32 year-old paralegal from Charlottesville, and injuring 19 others

The driver of the car, James Alex Fields, a 20 year-old from Ohio, and reported "Nazi sympathizer is arrested and charged with second degree murder, three counts of malicious wounding and failure to stop, begging the question why wasn't he charged with wounding all 19?

From his $35 MILLION dollar home –
golf resort – away from home -- golf membership
reportedly costs $350,000 --
in Bedminster, New Jersey, Trump tweets
**"…there is "equal blame for the violence on
both sides."**

Saturday, August 12, 7:39 AM. David
Duke: tweets, "Today will be a historic day
remembered as the moment everything changed,"

After one of Trump's tweets scolds the
white supremacists for their part in the violence,
David Duke tweets: "So, after decades of white-
Americans being targeted for discrimination and
anti-white hatred, we come together as a people,
and you((Trump) attack us?'

August 12, 2:03 PM. David Duke tweets:
"I would recommend you (Trump) take a good
look in the mirror & remember it was white
Americans who put you in the presidency, not
radical leftists."

August 12, 3:26 PM. Trump changes
spots for a press conference. "We condemn in
the strongest terms this egregious display of
hatred, bigotry, and **violence on many sides, on
many sides** …hatred, bigotry, and violence ---
It's been going on for a long time in our country
…Not Donald Trump. Not Barack Obama. It's
been going on for a long, long time …the
counter-protesters, those marching for the
proposition that all men are created equal –
they're part of the problem too."

(According to Trump's idiosyncratic
paranoid reasoning, Martin Luther King's march
to Selma Alabama reignited the Civil War.)

August 12. 4:23 PM. Trump now switches to "law & order" Charlottesville property owner Donald J. Trump" "What is vital now is a swift restoration of law and order and the protection of innocent lives." (Translation: "I own property in Charlottesville. Incidents like this must be stopped. Otherwise, my property values go down,")

August 12, 5:19 PM. Trump now goes presidential/political: "We must remember this truth. No matter our color, creed, religion, or political party, we are ALL AMERICANS FIRST." (Translation: I'm first, and when Americans are first -- I'm first of the firsts.")

August 12, 5:49 PM. Trump: "We will continue to follow developments in Charlottesville and will provide whatever assistance is needed. We are ready, willing and able." (But not so "ready, willing, and able" to leave his golf course vacation for Charlottesville.)

August 12, 6:50 PM Trump trying not to reveal he has just slipped into the Bedminster 7-11 and is reading a sympathy card tweets, "Deepest condolences to the families & fellow officers of the **VA State Police** who died today. You're all among the best this nation produces." (Thus spaketh 'law and order,' Conservative, Nixonian, Republican and World's Number One phony, lying, propagandist, politician Donald Trump. (Note the **emphasis on the VA State police who died in a helicopter crash co-incidental to the violence, and no sympathy for the murdered counter-protester, her family, or the injured counter-protesters.)**

August 12, 7:25 PM. Back in the greeting card section of the Bedminster drug store, Trump now finds the appropriate card which he tweets: "Condolences to the family of the young woman killed today and best regards to all those injured in Charlottesville, Virginia. So sad."

(Tacky. The young woman has a name – Heather Heyer – a civil rights activist – one of those you blame for the violence.)

August 14, 6:29 PM. Narcissistic Personality Disorder Donald, being Narcissistic Disorder Donald, blames the media for his major media malapropism – assigning equal blame for the violence to the armed white supremacists, neo-Nazis, *et al*, and those protesting the white supremacists, neo-Nazis, *et al* , tweets: "Made additional remarks on Charlottesville and realize once again that the Fake News will never be satisfied. Truly bad people!"

(Methinks the "bad" can be best seen in thy mirror, Donald.)

August 15, Trump speaks at a press conference: "There was hatred and violence on many sides …the alt left "bears some responsibility for the violence" in Charlottesville. **"Nobody wants to blame violence on both sides… what about the fact that the other side "came charging with clubs …you had a group on one side that was bad and you had a group on the other side that was also very violent. And nobody wants to say that, but I'll say it right now. You had a group on the other side that came charging in without a permit and they were very, very violent."**

Trump later opined, that the movement to remove Civil War statues and monuments had gone too far, arguing that because "Washington and Jefferson were slave owners, will their statues be torn down too.." (Yes, Donald, along with the Lincoln Memorial, for according to your extreme right wing "fake history" it was Lincoln who invaded the South and started the Civil War, in which 620,000 men died.

At the end, Trump boasted that he owned property in Charlottesville – a house and winery.

August 15, 4:45 PM. David Duke: tweets: "Thank you President Trump for your honesty & courage to tell the truth about Charlottesville & condemn the leftist terrorists in BLM/Antifa."

August 16, 10:56 AM. Trump turns presidential/political/exploitive:. "Memorial service today for beautiful and incredible Heather Heyer, a truly special young woman. She will be long remembered by all."(What fools still believe Trump was not the consummate Conservative politician?)

August 17, 6:19, 6:24, and 6:32 AM. Narcissistic Personality Disorder Trump turns envious: "Lindsey Graham falsely stated that I said there is moral equivalency between the KKK, neo-Nazi & white supremacist and people like Ms. Heyer. Such a disquieting Lie. He just can't forget his election trouncing. The people of South Carolina will remember. The public is learning (even more so) how dishonest the Fake News is. They totally misrepresent what I say about hate, bigotry etc., Shame!"

What is to be gleaned from the events in Charlottesville, VA on August 11-12., 2017, as to the person and presidency of Donald J. Trump?

First, Trump's world is constricted and restricted to preserve, protect and defend, his self-imposed grandiose delusion that he is Hitler's, not Nietzsche's, SUPERMAN – whose every word, tweet, and action is to prop up his delusion of superiority, *uber alles*, omniscient, omnipotent, deserving constant, unquestioned, and obsequious admiration, entitled to exploit events (Charlottesville) and persons (his base) in service of his grandiosity.

Committed to the proposition of infallibility, Trump must blame ("Fake News" & "voter fraud") for any and all criticism and anyone who questions his *ex cathedra* tweets must be dispatched with ruthless slander, insults, and character assassination.

The violence in Charlottesville on August 11-12, both exposed and encapsulated Trump's liability as President of the United States, incapacitated by a severe mental disorder which precludes him from responding outside that disorder – to act presidential as required for the public good in times of great need.

At a far more nefarious level, Trump's assigning "equal blame on both sides," **exposes the fatal flaw in Trump's presidency – his loyalty is to Donald J. Trump as Donald sees the world through the eyes of a Narcissistic Personality -- NOT to the United States, NOT to its Constitution, and NOT to all Americans.**

Trump does not, cannot, and will not act presidential, loyal to the United States and the Constitution, representing all its people, because being President is but a manifestation – an outgrowth – as natural a progression in the life of a Narcissistic Personality Disorder as pubic hair is to a 12 year-old.

Forced by the Charlottesville Affair to chose between duty to Country and all its citizens, or supporters sustaining Trump's delusions of grandeur by attending his rallies, Trump betrays Country for his base, choosing white supremacists, neo-Nazis, outlaw para-military hate groups, anti-Semites and anti-Muslims over ""those marching for the proposition that all men are created equal – they're part of the problem, too."

By inciting white-supremacists, neo-Nazis, neo-Nationalists, racists, KKK"ers, anti-Semites, anti-Muslims, Hillary and Obama haters – "Killer Hillary," "Convict Hillary," "Foreign-Born Obama," to acts of violence, Trump's fingerprints are on the steering wheel of the car that plowed into the crowd of "those marching for the proposition for the proposition that all men are created equal," killing Heather Heyer and injuring 19.

By "adhering" to those groups, who by their actions and pronouncements declare themselves to be enemies of the United States, and by giving these hate groups "aid and comfort within the United States," Trump is guilty of treason and "shall suffer death, or shall be imprisoned not less than five years … and shall be incapable of holding any office

under the United States .'' (18 U.S. Code # 2381 - Treason.)

<u>Closing Statement</u>

The evidence presented proves, beyond reasonable doubt: (1) Donald Trump, having exceeded the criteria necessary for a diagnosis of Narcissistic Personality Disorder, is in fact a Narcissistic Personality Disorder.

(2)Trump's disorder is both so debilitating and so pervasive as to render Trump incapable of "faithfully executing the Office of President of the United States.."

(3) Trump's disorder is both so debilitating and so pervasive as to render Trump incapable of "preserving, protecting and defending the Constitution.

(4) Trump's continuing Presidency poses a serious threat to the internal and external security of the citizens of the United States.

(5) Trump must therefore be removed from office.

(6) Trump fraudulently induced voters to vote for him by making promises he knew, or should have known, he couldn't and wouldn't keep, to wit, "I will Repeal and Replace Obamacare," "I will build a wall across the Mexican border and make México pay for it," and, "By bringing manufacturing jobs back to the US, I'm going to be the greatest jobs president God ever made," because said promises were the province of Congress, not the President.

(7) Trump fraudulently induced voters to vote for him by making statements and tweets he

knew, or should have known, were lies, to wit, "Killer Hillary," "Convict Hillary," "Obama wire-tapped my offices," and "Barack Obama was born in Kenya and raised in Indonesia and Hawaii."

(8) Trump fraudulently induced voters to vote for him by willfully and maliciously withholding his tax records, his bankruptcies, his foreign business dealings and holdings, and his past and present business and political contacts with Russians.

(9) Trump fraudulently induced voters to vote for him by willfully and maliciously misrepresenting that his business dealings and his non-political status qualified him for the presidency, when Trump knew he had no training, no experience, or no competence in governance, but had, in fact, been involved in politics for at least 20 years, including running for office.

(10) Trump fraudulently induced voters to vote for him by willfully and maliciously omitting the fact that he had obtained FIVE deferments to avoid serving in the Vietnam War, including a suspicious medical deferment, thereby misleading voters as to his integrity to be Commander-in-Chief,

(11) Trump fraudulently induced voters to vote for him by willfully and maliciously misrepresenting his political persuasion of a "Populist, "when the evidence of his vicious, specious, racist attacks on African-American President Obama, his slanderous claim that Obama's birth certificate was "forged, "Trump's personal, desperate compulsion to repeal and

replace Obamacare, his knee-jerk rescinding of all things Obama, Trump's personal congratulations to "Sheriff Joe" for his bogus investigation of Obama's birth certificate, his rush to deport and hunt and kill immigrants at the border, Trump's consistent pro-police/anti-protester bias, his support of the white supremacist, neo-Nazis; hate groups, and in Charlottesville, Virginia, and his Hitleresque/neo-nationalist speech to the United Nations, prove Trump's "Populist" claim to be a fraud – a ruse to exploit those who lost their homes and jobs due to Republican President Bush II's unregulated banks and mortgage companies.

(12) Trump's ambitions are NOT "Populist", but rather Neo-Nationalist to overthrow the Government of the United States as Hitler did in Germany in the 1930's.

Fraud vitiates the most solemn contracts, documents and even judgments -- everything, a judgment equally with a contract, " *US v. Throckmorton,* 98 U.S. 61 (1878).

"Fraud destroys the validity of everything into which it enters," *Nuddv. Burrows*, 91 U.S.436

"Fraud vitiates everything," *Biyce v. Grundy.* 3 Pet. 210.

"Out of fraud, no action arises. Fraud never gives a right of action. No court will lend its aid to a man who founds his cause of action upon an immoral or illegal act," Black's law Dictionary, Fifth Edition, Page 509.

"We have no officers in this government from the President down to the most subordinate agent, who does not hold office under the law

with prescribed duties and limited authority,"
Pierce v. United States, 7 Wall. (74 U.S.) 666-677.

To prevail in an action for fraud against Trump, it must be shown that Trump made the statements – he did, the statements were false – they were. Trump knew they were false, or made "recklessly without knowledge of its truth – Trump did both, that voters acted as if Trump's statements were true – they voted for Trump, and suffered injury and damages as a result – the Country is in an internecine war with itself.

"Therefore, Donald J. Trump's contract with the American voters and the United States. having been fraudulently obtained, must be "vitiated" – vacated -- as a matter of law, all Executive Orders, Laws Bills, Initiatives, Rules and Appointments made by President Trump must be voided because he never was the lawful President, and the person who finished second place in the election of 2016, be declared the winner and President of the United States.

The fundamental precept inherent in America's judicial system is that **NO PERSON IS ABOVE THE LAW!.**

On the other hand, Trump's insanity defense would lead to the same inexorable conclusion, if for a different reason – Trump must be removed from the Office of President of the United States. *

Raised by random humans, wannabe left fielder for Boston Red Sox. took six years to be only family member to graduate from college, Ph.D., UNC, published Dissertation in *JABA,* along with some 15 professional research studies, therapist in private practice, business owner, incurable whistle-blower, college professor, felicitous felon, dysfunctional dad, hapless husband x 4, and "late-bloomer" novelist -- *The Governor's Fingerprints,* true crime investigation - *Justice for Baby Josh* memoir, *Alice's Wonderland,* critiques of Bush II and Trump (2), family law-- *My Daughters Keeper, Good Dad Bad Mom, Parts 1 and 2 ,* myths of Judaism and Christianity – *God: Torah and Bible for Smart and Funny People Only,* the relationships of mothers and sons—*Johnny Carson, Ted Williams and Me*, and *Dirty Judges* -- an expose of criminal and corrupt judges in New Hampshire, Massachusetts, Florida, Virginia, and North Carolina – State & Federal Courts including US Supreme Court. (to be published in the spring.)